John C. Calhoun
A Bibliography

## Meckler's Bibliographies of American Notables

*Series Editor: Carol B. Fitzgerald*

1. John C. Calhoun: A Bibliography
   Clyde N. Wilson
   ISBN 0-88736-302-4   CIP   1990

2. Daniel Webster: A Bibliography
   Harold D. Moser
   ISBN 0-88736-712-7   CIP   *forthcoming*

# John C. Calhoun

A Bibliography

Clyde N. Wilson

BIBLIOGRAPHIES OF
AMERICAN NOTABLES, No. 1

Meckler
Westport • London

ROBERT MANNING
STROZIER LIBRARY

JUL 1 1 1991

TALLAHASSEE, FL'

**Library of Congress Cataloging-in-Publication Data**

Wilson, Clyde Norman.
   John C. Calhoun : a bibliography / Clyde N. Wilson.
     p.  cm. — (Meckler's bibliographies of American notables ; 1)
   Includes bibliographical references and indexes.
   ISBN 0-88736-302-4 : $   .
   1. Calhoun, John C. (John Caldwell), 1782–1850—Bibliography.
2. United States—Politics and government—1815–1861—Bibliography.
3. South Carolina—Politics and government—1775–1865—Bibliography.
I. Title.  II. Series.
Z8140.62.W55  1990
[E340.C15]
016.9735'092—dc20                                                 90-6508
                                                                                                                     CIP

**British Library Cataloguing in Publication Data**

Wilson, Clyde N.
   John C. Calhoun : a bibliography—(Bibliographies of
American notables; no. 1).
   1. United States. Politics. Calhoun, John C. (John
Caldwell) 1782–1850—Bibliographies
I. Title  II. Series
016.9735092

ISBN 0-88736-302-4

Copyright © 1990 Meckler Corporation. All rights reserved.
No part of this publication may be reproduced in any form
by any means without prior written permission from the publisher, except
by a reviewer who may quote brief passages in review.

Meckler Corporation, 11 Ferry Lane West, Westport, CT 06880.
Meckler Ltd., Grosvenor Gardens House, Grosvenor Gardens,
   London SW1W 0BS, U.K.

Printed on acid free paper.
Printed and bound in the United States of America.

# Contents

| | |
|---|---|
| Editor's Preface | ix |
| Introduction | 1 |
| Chronology: John Caldwell Calhoun | 7 |
| I.   Manuscript and Archival Resources | 11 |
|     A.  Unpublished Personal Papers | 11 |
|         1. Major Collections (1–2) | 11 |
|         2. Other Collections (3–26) | 11 |
|     B.  Published Personal Papers | 14 |
|         1. Major Collections (27–30) | 14 |
|         2. Other Publications (31–47) | 15 |
|     C.  Unpublished Official Papers | 17 |
|         1. In the South Carolina General Assembly, 1808–1810 (48) | 17 |
|         2. As U.S. Representative, 1811–1817 (49) | 17 |
|         3. As Secretary of War, 1817–1825 (50–67) | 17 |
|         4. As Vice President, 1825–1832 (68–69) | 19 |
|         5. As Senator, 1833–1843 (70) | 19 |
|         6. As Secretary of State, 1844–1845 (71–87) | 19 |
|         7. As Senator, 1845–1850 (88) | 21 |
|     D.  Published Official Papers | 21 |
|         1. As Secretary of War, 1817–1825 (89–93) | 21 |
|         2. As Secretary of State, 1844–1845 (94–104) | 21 |
|     E.  Unpublished Papers of Associates | 23 |
|         1. Major Collections (105–118) | 23 |
|         2. Other Collections with Significant Materials (119–136) | 25 |
|     F.  Published Papers of Associates | 27 |
|         1. Major Collections (137–141) | 27 |
|         2. Other Publications with Significant Material (142–168) | 27 |
|     G.  Contemporary Newspapers and Periodicals | 31 |
|         1. Newspapers (169–205) | 31 |

|     |     | 2. Periodicals (206–214) | 34 |
| --- | --- | --- | --- |
| II. | Speeches and Writings of John C. Calhoun | | 37 |
|     | A. Collections (215–219) | | 37 |
|     | B. Speeches | | 38 |
|     |     | 1. Collections (220–222) | 38 |
|     |     | 2. Compilations of Congressional Debates (223–227) | 38 |
|     |     | 3. Major Speeches | 39 |
|     |     |    a. In the U.S. House of Representatives, 1811–1817 (228–243) | 40 |
|     |     |    b. In the U.S. Senate, 1833–1843 (244–285) | 41 |
|     |     |    c. In the U.S. Senate, 1846–1850 (286–299) | 45 |
|     |     |    d. Other Speeches (Selected) (300–308) | 46 |
|     | C. Writings | | 47 |
|     |     | 1. Treatises | 47 |
|     |     |    a. The South Carolina Exposition (309–310) | 47 |
|     |     |    b. A Disquisition on Government (311–313) | 48 |
|     |     |    c. A Discourse on the Constitution and Government of the United States (314) | 48 |
|     |     | 2. Official Reports (Selected) | 48 |
|     |     |    a. In the U.S. House of Representatives, 1811–1817 (315–318) | 49 |
|     |     |    b. As Secretary of War, 1817–1825 (319–332) | 49 |
|     |     |    c. In the U.S. Senate, 1833–1843 (333–335) | 51 |
|     |     |    d. As Secretary of State, 1844–1845 (336–350) | 51 |
|     |     |    e. In the U.S. Senate, 1845–1850 (351) | 52 |
|     |     | 3. Essays, Articles, and Unofficial Reports (352–373) | 53 |
|     |     | 4. Public Letters (Selected) (374–383) | 55 |
| III. | Biographies of John C. Calhoun | | 57 |
|     | A. Books (384–396) | | 57 |
|     | B. Short Biographical Treatments (397–407) | | 58 |
| IV. | Background and Early Life (to 1811) | | 61 |
|     | A. The Calhouns and Related Families (408–420) | | 61 |
|     | B. Upcountry South Carolina (421–425) | | 62 |
|     | C. Early Life and Education (426–430) | | 63 |
|     | D. Yale College (431–436) | | 64 |
|     | E. Legal Education and Law Practice (437–444) | | 64 |
|     | F. South Carolina Politics in the Early Nineteenth Century (445–451) | | 65 |
|     | G. Calhoun's Public Life to 1811 (452–454) | | 66 |
| V. | Public Career of John C. Calhoun | | 67 |
|     | A. Historical Background | | 67 |
|     |     | 1. National Politics (455–467) | 67 |
|     |     | 2. The South (468–481) | 68 |
|     |     | 3. South Carolina | 70 |

## Contents

|  |  |
|---|---|
|       a. General (482–487) | 70 |
|       b. Politics (488–500) | 70 |
|       c. Economics (501–506) | 72 |
|       d. Society and Culture (507–512) | 73 |
|     4. Relevant Studies of Other States (513–518) | 73 |
|   B. U.S. House of Representatives, 1811–1817 | 74 |
|     1. General (519–524) | 74 |
|     2. The War of 1812 (525–531) | 75 |
|     3. Postwar Issues (532–536) | 75 |
|   C. Secretary of War, 1817–1825 | 76 |
|     1. The Monroe Cabinet and Administration (537–543) | 76 |
|     2. The War Department (544–554) | 77 |
|     3. Military Policy and Administration (555–567) | 78 |
|     4. Indian Policy and Administration (568–579) | 79 |
|     5. Miscellany (580–584) | 81 |
|   D. Presidential and Vice Presidential Candidacy, 1822–1824 (585–604) | 81 |
|   E. Vice President under Adams and Jackson, 1825–1832 | 83 |
|     1. The Adams Administration, 1825–1829 (605–614) | 83 |
|     2. The First Jackson Administration, 1829–1833 (615–622) | 85 |
|   F. The Nullification Episode, 1828–1833 | 86 |
|     1. Documents (623–630) | 86 |
|     2. Nullification as Doctrine (631–647) | 86 |
|     3. Nullification as Historical Episode (648–673) | 88 |
|   G. Senator, 1833–1843 | 91 |
|     1. General (674–683) | 91 |
|     2. National Issues (684–694) | 92 |
|     3. South Carolina Politics in the Post-Nullification Period (695–700) | 93 |
|   H. Presidential Candidacy, 1842–1844 (701–712) | 94 |
|   I. Secretary of State, 1844–1845 | 95 |
|     1. The Tyler Administration (713–717) | 95 |
|     2. The State Department and Diplomacy (718–730) | 96 |
|     3. Texas and Slavery (731–749) | 97 |
|     4. Other Issues (750–761) | 99 |
|   J. Senator, 1845–1850 | 101 |
|     1. General (762–770) | 101 |
|     2. The Crisis of 1850 and Its Aftermath (771–790) | 102 |
|     3. Selected Memorials (791–802) | 104 |
| VI. John C. Calhoun's Associates | 107 |
|   A. National Figures (803–835) | 107 |
|   B. South Carolinians (836–872) | 112 |
|   C. Lieutenants and Allies in Other States (873–893) | 117 |

|  |  |  |
|---|---|---|
| VII. | Personal Life of John C. Calhoun | 121 |
|  | A. General (894–901) | 121 |
|  | B. Wife, Children, Other Relatives, and Descendants (902–920) | 122 |
|  | C. Fort Hill and Pendleton (921–933) | 124 |
|  | D. The Calhoun Gold Mine (934–940) | 125 |
|  | E. Miscellany (941–948) | 126 |
|  | F. Selected First-hand Encounters (949–963) | 127 |
| VIII. | Historical Evaluation of John C. Calhoun | 129 |
|  | A. Public Career (964–997) | 129 |
|  | B. Political Thought | 133 |
|  |    1. Monographs (998–1002) | 133 |
|  |    2. Short General Treatments (1003–1022) | 133 |
|  |    3. Background (1023–1041) | 136 |
|  |    4. Contemporary and Later Defences of States Rights (1042–1052) | 138 |
|  |    5. Economics (1053–1062) | 139 |
|  |    6. Slavery (1063–1076) | 140 |
|  |    7. Miscellany (1077–1089) | 141 |
|  | C. Twentieth-Century Applications (1090–1123) | 143 |
|  | D. Oratorical and Literary Analysis (1124–1149) | 146 |
| IX. | Iconography | 151 |
|  | A. Portraits (1150–1154) | 151 |
|  | B. Daguerreotypes (1155–1157) | 151 |
|  | C. Sculpture (1158–1162) | 152 |
|  | D. Miscellany (1163–1170) | 152 |
| X. | Prospective Works (1171–1176) | 155 |
| XI. | Indexes | 157 |
|  | Author Index | 157 |
|  | Subject Index | 165 |
|  | Serial Publications | 171 |

# Editor's Preface

Underneath all, individuals,
I swear nothing is good to me now that ignores individuals,
The American compact is altogether with individuals,
The only government is that which makes minute of individuals.

Walt Whitman
"By Blue Ontario's Shores"
1855

In the little more than 200 years since its independence, the United States has left an indelible mark on man's history. There is endless debate about the unique combination of circumstances that encouraged the development of the country, but the results are clear. This country has nurtured leadership in all areas of human thought.

The booklength bibliographies in this series seek to honor some of the notable contributors to American civilization in the sciences and social sciences. Those to be included will be innovators in social, economic, or political theory and practice, or scientific invention. Some will have reshaped traditional ideas for new application. Others may be best known as commentators who interpret the American scene. Eminent subject specialists will gather and annotate citations by and about the person, from his or her own writings, and manuscript collections, monographs, articles, dissertations, theses, and oral history as available. Government documents, technical reports, and other special resources will be noted where appropriate. Each volume will follow a uniform format, including a detailed subject index.

The bibliographers in the series will identify and describe the available narrative and critical research on the notable. The discerning reader will see what remains to be studied for a fuller understanding of the individual's contribution to American culture.

*Carol Bondhus Fitzgerald*

*John C. Calhoun, 1843. An engraving by John Sartain from a miniature portrait by James Wise. Courtesy of the South Caroliniana Library, University of South Carolina.*

# Introduction

John C. Calhoun has a somewhat unique position in American history. For four decades, during a critical period of American development, he was a political figure of national power and prominence and held most of the high offices of the federal government. He was never the leader of a national party like Martin Van Buren or Henry Clay, never president like John Quincy Adams, never the beneficiary of widespread popularity like Andrew Jackson, never predominant in influence, even in the South, but he always had to be taken into account. From the beginning to the end of his career (from 1811 to 1850) he had an influence on every issue and aspect of national politics, and not merely on the questions of state rights and slavery with which his name is most commonly associated. He became, though this was not fully consummated until after his death, the political genius of the South, and thus a major protagonist in the drama of sectional conflict which is the heart and center of American history in the 19th century. Whatever road one travels, observed V. L. Parrington, correctly, a half century ago (#1018), one finds Calhoun standing at the crossroads.

During the War of 1812, while still in his early thirties, his leadership in the House of Representatives was such that a prominent editor called him "the young Hercules who carried the war on his shoulders." In 1824, at the age of 42, he was elected vice president of the United States by a large majority without the direct backing of any presidential ticket and with as much northern as southern support. He was the youngest man to be elected president or vice president and the first who was not from Virginia, New York, or Massachusetts.

Characterized, strangely, as an "opportunist" by one biographer (#384), he in 1832 resigned the vice presidency to lead his own small state in defiance of the executive and legislative branches of the federal government, the Democratic and Whig parties, overwhelming public opinion, and the formidable popularity and temper of Andrew Jackson. Though "nullification" has often been characterized as suicidal or absurd, and Calhoun's most recent biographer (#392) has described him as being "out of touch with reality," the upshot was that Calhoun

1

and South Carolina fought all the powers arrayed against them down to a compromise of the crisis, no small feat for a public figure out of touch with reality.

Within a few years Calhoun was once more virtually the leader of the Democratic party in the Senate and a presidential contender. At this time, his quite substantial body of followers in the Democratic party in the North were described as "young men and . . . those of advanced views in politics who were generally independent in thought and action" (#712). A few years after that a weak and beleaguered "accidental" President, John Tyler, was faced with a sudden vacancy in the State Department at a time which everyone recognized was crucial in foreign relations, with the issues of Texas and Oregon coming to a point. Tyler, without Calhoun's knowledge, sent his name to the Senate as secretary of state. The nomination was approved in a matter of hours, without a single recorded dissent, Democrat or Whig, Northern or Southern.

All this is to indicate that Calhoun played a larger role in his times than common report, focusing on the slavery controversy, has allowed. But in addition to this, Calhoun has another significance that is not shared by most public figures of the same stature in his own time and later. A surprisingly large number of observers, from diverse generations, countries, and viewpoints, have found him to be a political thinker of permanent interest. While Calhoun is very far from being the most admired of American statesmen, he has never at any time lacked weighty admirers. And except for Jefferson and Lincoln, it is hard to think of any American statesman who has had admirers from more diverse points of the compass and the political spectrum, and for reasons that transcend the issues of his own time.

Historical evaluations of Calhoun tend to fall into two schools, both of which date back to Calhoun's own lifetime. One school is attracted by his intellect and character, the tragic nobility of his career, and the timeless elements of his political thought. This school crested in the 1950s and has had a minor revival in the 1980s. It began in Calhoun's lifetime and has never died entirely away. The other school portrays him as either deluded or fanatical, or both, warped by ambition and unrealistic abstractionism. This view originates in contemporary journalistic criticism and has continued to the present.

Students who wish to look into Calhoun's career should be aware that the literature does not progress according to an orderly scholarly paradigm. Scholarship is generally assumed to be cumulative and progressive. More and more is learned, the issues are clarified, and questions are debated within a narrowing range. Such is most definitely not the case with Calhoun. The literature does not so much progress as go round in circles, and large gaps remain in our knowledge. Nor

# Introduction

can it be assumed that recent literature is in any sense more reliable than older writings.

A Calhoun bibliography necessarily reflects these factors. It is necessary to gather materials from a host of different, varied, and even odd sources. Primary sources of all sorts must be looked at afresh, and these often display unfortunate lacunae. For instance Calhoun's early life, up until the time he entered Congress in 1811, is sparsely documented for a figure of such importance, and it is not until the early 1830s, when he began to preserve his papers systematically, that a record exists that is really satisfactory in detail. Where primary sources are lacking, secondary materials are necessarily thin.

Also, a large variety of collateral sources must be consulted, including both popular and scholarly literature of the late 19th and early 20th centuries and of more recent times, both on Calhoun and on subjects in which he was involved, in the treatment of which he too often appears tangentially or superficially. Many items included in this bibliography, then, represent not definitive treatments of particular aspects of Calhoun's career, but bits and pieces of relevant data that still need to be pieced together.

Perhaps superficiality is the greatest problem, for many writers have assumed that Calhoun has already been adequately characterized, and they need do no more than refer to an accepted stereotype. Other writers have constantly discovered new aspects of his career and new applications of his political thought. There appears to have been little interchange between the two groups, and the first has hardly noticed the existence of the second.

An example of the first group is a work (#620) on the Jacksonian era by a well-known historian. According to this account (p. 184): "John C. Calhoun never ceased grinding his teeth over" the fact that he had been double-crossed by Martin Van Buren on the Tariff of 1828. In fact, Calhoun was a man of great strength and poise who never ground his teeth over anything. The physical image of Calhoun grinding his teeth is, of course, a put-down circulated by his enemies at the time, which finds its way into the history books as a fact.

Again, we are told (p. 167) that Calhoun had only to blame his "own foolish mistakes" for his falling out with Andrew Jackson and losing the presidential succession. In fact, the actions referred to were neither foolish nor mistaken, but a deliberate choice made in full understanding of the consequences. They were "foolish mistakes" not in objective fact but in the perception of politicians who regarded the kind of pragmatic self-interest that Calhoun eschewed as a norm.

The point is not to criticize one book, but to warn the reader that a great deal of the literature that refers to Calhoun is of such a nature. It persists because it is assumed, rightly, that the reader will quite often already have in mind a negative stereotype of Calhoun that will be activated.

The leading historian of American banking (#688) has stated that Calhoun understood fiscal and monetary questions better than any statesman of the time. He certainly made many more speeches about currency and banking, trade and taxation, the public lands, and other economic subjects than he did about slavery. But aside from a work in Italian (#998) and an obscure dissertation (#1054), there is no booklength study of Calhoun's political economy. And though he was secretary of state at a crucial time and played an important role in the War of 1812, the Mexican War, and the Texas and Oregon questions, the only systematic study of his foreign policy is a dissertation at a Swiss university (#725).

But more disheartening than the lack of crucial studies is the failure of those who write on Calhoun to make use of what exists, or even to recognize neglected issues. The most recent biography, mentioned earlier, does not even acknowledge the existence of such issues or show any recognition of their importance at the time. In this biography internal improvements, the currency, the public lands, are of no concern except in the most trivial sense as political tactics. There is no awareness that Calhoun had a fully developed political economy that differed from those of both the Democratic and Whig parties and had a substantial number of adherents.

This particular biography, which is published by a respectable university press and which has received an award, treats Calhoun as a warped personality and with no recognition of the role he really played in his times. Yet it has been called by several reviewers a sympathetic biography. One wonders what the reviewers would have thought was an unsympathetic biography. In fact, this work and some others that could be mentioned are self-negating. Nowhere in the book can we get any understanding of why so deluded and failed a figure is worthy of yet another biography, all of which merely indicates the degree to which unthinking stereotypes dominate much of the literature.

I am not complaining that these works are hostile, but that they are superficial. Calhoun was a controversial figure who stood against the course that American history has taken, and hostility is inevitable. There are any number of hostile treatments that take him seriously and have significant things to say (#393, 999, 1000, 1009, for instance). A quite hostile biography of a century ago (#386), however, deals more seriously with the issues of Calhoun's time than the most recent one. Calhoun simply cannot be accounted for if treated merely as a conventional short-sighted politician who deluded himself and failed. This is to miss not only the great influence he exercised over the

# Introduction

public life of his own time, but also the strong intellectual and ethical purchase he had on the traditions of American republicanism and thus the influence that his ideas and arguments have had on later generations.

The potential reader should by now be warned that the secondary work on Calhoun does not make for an orderly progression with clearly defined issues. For Calhoun many of the issues are still undefined and the evaluations swing so widely that they do not even achieve any overlap. Possibly this itself is a measure of his importance and of the ambiguity with which Americans still approach some of the central issues of their history.

A work like this bibliography will presumably be used by two different types of readers—beginning students looking into the subject for the first time, and more advanced and specialized scholars seeking sources on particular points. I would advise the beginning student to look first at one of the better short biographical articles that are readily available (#403 or #407). Then proceed to Margaret L. Coit's Pulitzer Prize winning biography (#385), still the best one-volume treatment. If further information is needed, the student can move on to Charles M. Wiltse's three-volume definitive work (#396), which covers all aspects of Calhoun's career better than any other extant biography. Then, it might be worthwhile to study this bibliography for further clues and to look at some of Calhoun's own writings in #30 or #215.

For the more advanced student, this book will be as useful for what does not appear (because it does not exist) as for what appears herein. I would advise the researcher to study the organization of this bibliography, take note of the scanty and inadequate representation in some areas, and the radical disagreements among authors. If he is wise he will find numerous clues to research papers that have not yet been done—research that will contribute not only to the understanding of Calhoun but to aspects of the whole great middle period of American history in which he acted.

Despite the inadequacies of the literature, its production has been continuous throughout the 20th century. Nowhere has this diverse material been brought together and accounted for in one place. Until recently it would hardly have been possible. But, given modern facilities for reproduction and exchange of bibliographic information, and the several decades of accumulation of material that have gone into the ongoing publication of a 25-volume edition of *The Papers of John C. Calhoun* (#30) at the University of South Carolina, it is now possible. The completion of this project could not have been accomplished without the work that has been carried out over the years by a number of members of the editorial staff of the *Calhoun Papers,* especially

Alexander Moore, assistant editor, who has worked resourcefully on the Calhoun secondary bibliography. As always, Associate Editor Shirley B. Cook has provided me indispensable help.

Because of his importance, his dramatic career, and the interest of later generations in his ideas, Calhoun is likely always to remain a significant subject in American historical writing. This gathering of materials marks an important step in the dissemination of knowledge and the furthering of future scholarship and understanding. It is pleasing that the occasion and opportunity has been provided to compile and publish it.

Clyde N. Wilson<br>
Columbia, S.C.

# Chronology: John Caldwell Calhoun

| | |
|---|---|
| *18 March 1782* | Born at Long Canes settlement, Abbeville District, South Carolina. Family on both sides were Scotch-Irish, among the earliest settlers of the South Carolina upcountry, and Revolutionary patriots. Grew up on family plantations, largely self-educated. |
| *1795* | Student at Moses Waddel's academy. |
| *1800* | Again at Waddel's academy. |
| *1802–1804* | At Yale College, entering as a junior. |
| *1804–1806* | Studies law at Charleston and at the Litchfield Law School, Connecticut. |
| *1807–1811* | Practices law in upcountry South Carolina and serves in two sessions of the state legislature. |
| *8 January 1811* | Marries Floride Bonneau Colhoun. They have 10 children, seven of whom survive him. |
| *1811–1817* | In the U.S. House of Representatives from South Carolina. Enters as a "War Hawk" and soon becomes a leading member and chairman of the Foreign Relations Committee. During the War of 1812 serves so ably as a debater and legislator that he is referred to as "the young Hercules who carried the war on his shoulders." In 1816 plays a leading role in legislation for the peacetime military establishment, for chartering the second Bank of the United States, and for a national program of internal improvements, to be paid for by non-tax revenues. |

| | |
|---|---|
| *1817–1825* | Secretary of war in the cabinet of President James Monroe. Resolves the immense financial confusion left by the war; reforms the supply, engineering, medical, and Indian administrations, and West Point. Resides on the Georgetown estate later known as "Dumbarton Oaks" and with his family plays a prominent role in Washington society. |
| *1822–1823* | Is promoted in diverse quarters as a candidate for the presidency to succeed Monroe—in competition with his Cabinet mates John Quincy Adams and William H. Crawford, Speaker Henry Clay, and General Andrew Jackson. Withdraws when the Pennsylvania nomination goes to Jackson. |
| *1824* | Elected vice president of the U.S. by a sizable majority while the presidential election is split four ways and has to be decided by the House of Representatives in favor of Adams, amidst cries of "corrupt bargain." |
| *1825–1829* | First term as vice president, under Adams. Differs with the president and, with his supporters in Congress, joins the coalition behind Jackson. |
| *1826* | Settles in the western corner of South Carolina and begins developing "Fort Hill" plantation (later the campus of Clemson University), a few miles from the town of Pendleton, which is his home for the rest of his life. |
| *1828* | Re-elected vice president on Jackson's ticket. Writes anonymously for the South Carolina legislature the "South Carolina Exposition" which outlines the injustice and unconstitutionality of the Tariff of 1828 ("Tariff of Abominations") and suggests a remedy—state interposition, called by critics "nullification." This document is broadcast but not immediately acted upon. |
| *1829–1832* | Second term as vice president, under Jackson. Strained relations develop between the president and vice president over the social status of Mrs. John H. Eaton, over the actions of South Carolina and Jackson's failure to support significant tariff |

## Chronology: John Caldwell Calhoun

| | |
|---|---|
| | reform, and over Jackson's objection to Calhoun's criticism of him during the Seminole War of 1818—when Calhoun had been his superior. |
| *17 February 1831* | Calhoun makes public his separation from the president by publishing his position on the Seminole War controversy. Most of the cabinet resigns in support of Calhoun. |
| *26 July 1831* | Calhoun publicly defends the South Carolina doctrine of "interposition" by his "Fort Hill Address." |
| *24 November 1832* | A plenary convention of the people of South Carolina passes an ordinance nullifying the federal tariff laws, to take effect the following February. |
| *10 December 1832* | Jackson issues a proclamation suggesting that nullification will be put down as treason. |
| *28 December 1832* | Calhoun resigns as vice president, having two weeks before been elected to fill an unexpired term as senator from South Carolina. |
| *January–March 1833* | Calhoun joins the Senate, vigorously defends his state, but works for a legislative compromise to end the crisis. Congress passes a bill upholding the enforcement of federal laws and another providing for the gradual reduction of tariff rates. Calhoun returns to South Carolina and secures repeal of the Nullification ordinance. The "compromise of 1833" is complete. |
| *1833–1843* | Senator from South Carolina. During 1833–1838 Calhoun, with a small following in Congress, maintains a position independent of both Whig and Democratic parties. He outlines distinct positions on banking and currency, tariff and free trade, revenue, public lands, and reform of the "spoils" system. Begins to take a hard line against the rising tide of abolitionist sentiment. From 1839 he rejoins the Democratic party, supports Martin Van Buren's unsuccessful bid for re-election, and takes a leading role among Democrats in Congress, after the Whig victory in 1840, in opposing the nationalistic Whig legislative program. Resigns 3 March 1843. |

| | |
|---|---|
| *1842–1844* | Is promoted in South Carolina, some other Southern states, and in New York as a candidate for the Democratic presidential nomination in 1844. |
| *January 1844* | Withdraws his name from consideration by the Democratic National Convention, objecting to the structure of the convention and the waffling of party leaders on Texas annexation, the tariff, and abolitionism. |
| *6 March 1844* | Without his knowledge is nominated by President John Tyler to be secretary of state. Confirmed the same day by the Senate with no recorded dissent. |
| *1 April 1844—10 March 1845* | Secretary of state. Negotiates a treaty for the annexation of the Texas Republic to the U.S. which is rejected by the Senate; the objective is accomplished later, after the election of 1844, by the admission of Texas to the Union as a state. Pursues negotiations with the British for the peaceful division of the Oregon Territory, which progress but are not brought to a conclusion. Vigorously objects to British efforts to interfere with slavery in the Americas. |
| *1845–1850* | Again in the Senate. Refuses to vote for the Mexican War, which he believes has been brought on by unconstitutional presidential action, has no legitimate goals, and will lead to sectional conflict. Opposes the Polk administration's jingoism in Oregon and Mexico. During his last years works with limited success to achieve Southern unity in Congress, above party loyalties. This, he believes, is the only way to preserve both the South and the Union. Opposes the "Compromise of 1850" as inadequate for the South and not a real settlement. Predicts civil war in the future. |
| *31 March 1850* | Dies in Washington. Buried at St. Philip's Episcopal Church, Charleston. |
| *1853* | Richard K. Crallé publishes *A Disquisition on Government* and *A Discourse on the Constitution and Government of the United States,* which Calhoun had left in manuscript. |

# I.
# Manuscript and Archival Resources

### A. UNPUBLISHED PERSONAL PAPERS

**1. Major Collections**

**1.** Clemson, S.C., Clemson University. John C. Calhoun Papers, 1805–1850. 2,500 items. The basic collection of papers retained by Calhoun and his immediate family at Fort Hill plantation during the last 25 years of his life.

**2.** Columbia, S.C., South Caroliniana Library, University of South Carolina. John C. Calhoun Papers, 1801–1899. 3,500 items. Extensive collection of correspondence and other papers of Calhoun and close relatives, gathered from many sources. Collection continues to grow.

**2. Other Collections**

In addition to the two major collections listed above, approximately 75 repositories (other than official archives) hold one or more manuscript groups containing from one to several dozen Calhoun manuscripts each. These are primarily, though not entirely, letters from Calhoun to many different individuals. Some of the larger and more coherent of these collections are listed below. The edition of *The Papers of John C. Calhoun* (#30) presents a complete chronological publication of all known documents (except minor administrative correspondence). It should be noted that most of the manuscript groups which have been listed under "E. Unpublished Papers of Associates" contain many Calhoun letters and other Calhoun documents as well as material about Calhoun. Numerous collections that are smaller, less coherent, or less significant are not cited.

**3.** Ann Arbor, Mich., University of Michigan, William L. Clements Library. Christopher Vandeventer Papers. Series of personal letters from Calhoun, 1816–1838, to Vandeventer who was his chief clerk in the War Department.

**4.** Austin, Texas, University of Texas, Barker Texas History Center. John C. Calhoun papers in various collections. A considerable number of letters in various collections, chiefly concerned with the Texas annexation period, 1844–1845.

**5.** Boston, Massachusetts Historical Society. Marcus Morton Letterbooks. Series of letters to Calhoun from an important Massachusetts Democratic politician, 1818–1846.

**6.** Charleston, S.C., Charleston Library Society. John C. Calhoun Papers. Series of 18 letters, 1844–1850, from Calhoun to Henry W. Conner of Charleston.

**7.** Chicago, Chicago Historical Society. Ninian Edwards Papers. Series of Calhoun letters to an Illinois political leader, 1818–1831.

**8.** Columbia, S.C., University of South Carolina, South Caroliniana Library. Thomas Waties Papers. A small collection of papers from Calhoun's law practice, 1809–1810.

**9.** Durham, N.C., Duke University. John C. Calhoun Papers, 1765–1892. 343 items. Mostly letters from Calhoun to various individuals, including significant series addressed to Armistead Burt, a South Carolina congressman and nephew by marriage; to Andrew Pickens [Jr.], a cousin and governor of South Carolina; to other relatives; and to the Rev. John D. Gardiner, a New York clergyman and Yale classmate. Also a significant number of Calhoun letters in many other collections.

**10.** Montgomery, Ala., Alabama Department of Archives and History. Bolling Hall Papers. Series of Calhoun letters to a Georgia and Alabama political leader, 1831–1835.

**11.** Montgomery, Ala., Alabama Department of Archives and History. Charles Tait Papers. Series of Calhoun letters to a Georgia and Alabama political leader, 1818–1821.

**12.** New Haven, Conn., Yale University, Sterling Library. John C. Calhoun papers in various collections. More than 70 items, mostly letters from Calhoun to many different individuals, with a few student

# Manuscript and Archival Resources 13

records and other materials. Also, a smaller amount of material in the Beinecke Library, Western Americana Collection.

**13.** New York, Pierpont Morgan Library. Henry Wheaton Papers. Series of Calhoun letters, 1816–1846, to a major American diplomat and scholar with whom he had a long and cordial relationship.

**14.** Philadelphia, Historical Society of Pennsylvania. John C. Calhoun papers in various collections. Approximately 150 letters to and from Calhoun and many different individuals in groups of personal papers and autograph collections.

**15.** Princeton, N.J., Princeton University. Richard Rush Papers. Series of letters, 1818–1848, to a Pennsylvania political leader and diplomat. (Published microfilm available.)

**16.** Princeton, N.J., Princeton University. Samuel L. Southard Papers. Series of personal letters to a colleague in the Monroe cabinet.

**17.** San Marino, Cal., Huntington Library. Francis Lieber Papers. Small series of Calhoun letters to a political scientist.

**18.** Washington, Library of Congress, Manuscripts Division. John C. Calhoun Papers, 1819–1850, *ca.* 50 items. Primarily letters from Calhoun to a variety of persons, collected from different sources. Includes important series of letters to Littleton W. Tazewell, a Virginia political leader, and to John R. Mathewes, a friend in private life. (See #29)

**19.** Washington, Library of Congress, Manuscripts Division. Carnegie Institution of Washington Transcript Collection. Includes over 60 Calhoun related items, many not known in any other source. (See #29)

**20.** Washington, Library of Congress, Manuscripts Division. Andrew Jackson Donelson Papers. Letters of Calhoun to the nephew of Andrew Jackson who was U.S. Minister to Texas while Calhoun was secretary of state. (Published microfilm available.)

**21.** Washington, Library of Congress, Manuscripts Division. Thomas Jefferson Papers. About 15 items between Jefferson and Calhoun, 1817–1825. (Presidential Papers Microfilm.)

**22.** Washington, Library of Congress, Manuscripts Division. James MacBride Papers. Small but important early series of letters, 1811–1813, from Calhoun to a Yale classmate. (See #29)

**23.** Washington, Library of Congress, Manuscripts Division. John McLean Papers. Series of letters from Calhoun to an Ohio politician, 1827–1829. (See #29)

**24.** Washington, Library of Congress, Manuscripts Division. Henry R. Schoolcraft Papers. Correspondence between Calhoun and an Indian Agent in the Northwest. (See #29)

**25.** Washington, Library of Congress, Manuscripts Division. Samuel Smith Papers. Series of letters, 1818–1829, to a leading Maryland politician. (See #29)

**26.** Washington, Library of Congress, Manuscripts Division. Christopher Vandeventer Papers. Series of letters from Calhoun, 1819–1836. (See #29)

## B. PUBLISHED PERSONAL PAPERS

### 1. Major Collections

**27.** *Correspondence Addressed to John C. Calhoun, 1837–1849.* Edited by Chauncey S. Boucher and Robert P. Brooks. In *American Historical Association Annual Report* for 1929, pp. 125–570. Washington: U.S. Government Printing Office, 1930. Collection of political correspondence to Calhoun, from the Clemson University manuscripts and designed to supplement #28.

**28.** *Correspondence of John C. Calhoun.* Edited by J. Franklin Jameson. In *American Historical Association Annual Report* for 1899, vol. 2, 2 parts. Washington: U.S. Government Printing Office, 1900. A large collection of political correspondence to and from Calhoun, chiefly from the Clemson University manuscripts, but also including material in private hands.

**29.** *Microfilm of John C. Calhoun Papers in the Library of Congress.* Six reels. Washington: National Archives and Records Service, 1954. Pictures manuscript letters to and from Calhoun discovered as of the date of filming in about 40 different collections of personal papers in the Manuscripts Division of the Library of Congress.

## Manuscript and Archival Resources

**30.** *The Papers of John C. Calhoun.* Edited by Robert L. Meriwether, W. Edwin Hemphill, and Clyde N. Wilson. 19 vols. to date (covering 1801–1844) of a projected 25-vol. edition. Columbia, S.C.: University of South Carolina Press, 1959–. Comprehensive chronological publication of correspondence, writings, speeches, official documents, and other papers, from all known sources. Each volume contains notes, interpretive introduction, and exhaustive index.

### 2. Other Publications

**31.** Brownson, Henry F. *Orestes Brownson's Early Life: From 1803 to 1844.* Detroit: H.F. Brownson, publisher, 1898. Five letters from Calhoun.

**32.** "Calhoun-Gouverneur Correspondence, 1823–1836." *New York Public Library Bulletin* 3 (August 1899):324–333. Letters between Calhoun and James Monroe's son-in-law, chiefly about the Seminole War controversy.

**33.** [Cleveland, John B., ed.] *Controversy between John C. Calhoun and Robt. Y. Hayne as to the Proper Route of a Railroad from South Carolina to the West.* [Spartanburg, S.C.: privately printed, 1913.] A major internal controversy in South Carolina over the route to be taken by a projected railroad to the Ohio Valley.

**34.** Davis, Curtis Carroll. *That Ambitious Mr. Legaré: Life of James M. Legaré.* Columbia, S.C.: University of South Carolina Press, 1971. Three letters exchanged by Calhoun and an aspiring poet, 1847.

**35.** Flippin, Percy Scott, ed. "Herschel V. Johnson Correspondence." *North Carolina Historical Review* 4 (April 1927): 182–201. Includes six letters to Calhoun in his later years from a rising Georgia politician.

**36.** Hay, Thomas R., ed. "John C. Calhoun and the Presidential Campaign of 1824: Some Unpublished Calhoun Letters." *American Historical Review* 40 (October 1934): 82–96, and (January 1935): 287–300.

**37.** Jackman, Sydney W., ed. "John C. Calhoun to David Bates Douglass." *South Carolina Historical Magazine* 60 (April 1959). 83–85. To a West Point professor.

**38.** "John C. Calhoun to Thomas W. Gilmer." *William and Mary Quarterly,* 1st series 20 (July 1911): 8–10. On the annexation of Texas.

**39.** Lathers, Richard. *Reminiscences of Richard Lathers. Sixty Years of a Busy Life in South Carolina, Massachusetts and New York.* Edited by Alvan F. Sanborn. New York: The Grafton Press, 1907. Calhoun anecdotes and letters collected by an ubiquitous contemporary.

**40.** "Letters from John C. Calhoun to Francis W. Pickens." *South Carolina Historical Magazine* 7 (1906): 12–19. To a kinsman and political lieutenant in the 1840s.

**41.** Moltmann, Gunter, ed. "Eine Deutschland-Korrespondenz John C. Calhouns aus dem Jahre 1844." *Jahrbuch für Amerikastudien* 14 (1969): 155–168. Friendly unofficial correspondence with the Prussian minister to the U.S., Friedrich Ludwig von Röenne.

**42.** Newsome, Albert Ray, ed. "Correspondence of John C. Calhoun, George McDuffie and Charles Fisher, Relating to the Presidential Campaign of 1824." *North Carolina Historical Review* 7 (October 1930): 477–504. McDuffie was an important lieutenant in South Carolina and Fisher in North Carolina.

**43.** Owen, Thomas M., ed. "Letters from John C. Calhoun to Charles Tait." *Gulf States Historical Magazine* 1 (September 1902): 92–104. Candid private letters to a friend, a former representative from Georgia.

**44.** Sanders, George N. *The Political Correspondence of the Late Hon. George N. Sanders, Confederate Commissioner to Europe During the Civil War.* New York: American Art Association, [1914]. Four letters exchanged by Calhoun and a Kentucky fire-eater in the 1840s.

**45.** Upshur, John A., ed. "Letter of A.P. Upshur to J.C. Calhoun." *William and Mary Quarterly,* 2nd series 16 (October 1936): 554–557. On Texas annexation.

**46.** *The Voice of Truth, Containing General Joseph Smith's Correspondence with Gen. James Arlington Bennett; Appeal to the Green Mountain Boys; Correspondence with John C. Calhoun, Esq. . . .* Nauvoo, Ill.: John Taylor, 1844. Correspondence with the Mormon leader.

**47.** Waring, Alice Noble, ed. "Letters of John C. Calhoun to Patrick Noble, 1812–1837." *Journal of Southern History* 16 (February 1950): 64–74. Letters to a cousin.

**Manuscript and Archival Resources** 17

## C. UNPUBLISHED OFFICIAL PAPERS

### 1. In the South Carolina General Assembly, 1808–1810

**48.** Columbia, S.C., South Carolina Department of Archives and History. Records of the General Assembly, Committee Reports. A few papers relating to Calhoun's service in the S.C. House of Representatives.

### 2. As U.S. Representative, 1811–1817

**49.** Washington, National Archives. Record Group 233: Records of the U.S. House of Representatives, 12th–15th Congresses. Bills, committee reports, resolutions, and a few other documents.

### 3. As Secretary of War, 1817–1825

**50.** Washington, Library of Congress, Manuscripts Division. Jacob Brown Papers. Extensive correspondence between Secretary of War Calhoun and one of the ranking generals of the army. (See #29)

**51.** Washington, Library of Congress, Manuscripts Division. Thomas Sidney Jessup Papers. Papers of the Quartermaster General of the Army under Calhoun. (See #29)

**52.** Washington, National Archives. Record Group 46: Records of the U.S. Senate, 15th–18th Congresses. Reports of the secretary of war to Congress.

**53.** Washington, National Archives. Record Group 59: General Records of the Department of State. Letters of Application and Recommendation During the Administration of James Monroe, 1817–1825. (National Archives Microcopy 439.)

Washington, National Archives. Record Group 75: Records of the Bureau of Indian Affairs, in the following series:

**54.** Letters Received by the Office of Indian Affairs. (National Archives Microcopy 234.)

**55.** Letters Sent by the Secretary of War Relating to Indian Affairs. (Microcopy 15.)

**56.** Documents Relating to the Negotiation of Ratified and Unratified Indian Treaties. (Microcopy T-494.)

Washington, National Archives. Record Group 94: Records of the Adjutant General's Office, in the following series:

**57.** Letters Received by the Adjutant General's Office, Main Series. (National Archives Microcopies 566 and 567.)

**58.** Letters Sent by the Adjutant General's Office. (Microcopy 565.)

**59.** U.S. Military Academy: Application Papers of Cadets. (Microcopy 688.)

**60.** Records Relating to the U.S. Military Academy. (Microcopy 91.)

Washington, National Archives. Record Group 107: Records of the Office of the Secretary of War, in the following series:

**61.** Letters Received by the Secretary of War, Registered Series. (National Archives Microcopy 221.)

**62.** Letters Received by the Secretary of War, Unregistered Series. (Microcopy 222.)

**63.** Letters Sent by the Secretary of War Relating to Military Affairs. (Microcopy 6.)

**64.** Reports to Congress from the Secretary of War. (Microcopy 220.)

**65.** Confidential and Unofficial Letters Sent by the Secretary of War. (Microcopy 7.)

**66.** Letters Sent to the President by the Secretary of War. (Microcopy 127.)

**67.** Washington, National Archives. Record Group 233: Records of the U.S. House of Representatives, 15th–18th Congresses. Reports of the secretary of war to Congress.

**Manuscript and Archival Resources** 19

### 4. As Vice President, 1825–1832

**68.** Washington, National Archives. Record Group 46: Records of the U.S. Senate, 19th–22nd Congresses. There are no papers of the vice president as such, but there is a fair amount of material in the Senate records, chiefly minor administrative correspondence and petitions addressed to the president of the Senate.

**69.** Washington, National Archives. Record Group 59: General Records of the Department of State. Letters of Application and Recommendation During the Administration of Andrew Jackson, 1828–1837. (National Archives Microcopy 639.)

### 5. As Senator, 1833–1843

**70.** Washington, National Archives. Record Group 46: Records of the U.S. Senate, 22nd–27th Congresses. Bills, resolutions, committee reports, and other documents.

### 6. As Secretary of State, 1844–1845

**71.** Austin, Texas, Texas State Library. Records of the Texas Republic Department of State, U.S. Diplomatic Correspondence. Much correspondence between the Texan representatives in Washington and the Texas government, 1844–1845.

**72.** Berkeley, Calif., University of California, Bancroft Library. Thomas O. Larkin Papers. Letters between the secretary of state and the first U.S. consul in California, who took office under Calhoun.

**73.** Boston, Massachusetts Historical Society. Edward Everett Papers. Correspondence between Everett as U.S. minister to Great Britain and Calhoun as secretarty of state, and other items. (Published microfilm available.)

**74.** London, British Museum. Aberdeen Papers. Letters from the British minister to the U.S., Richard Pakenham, to the British foreign secretary concerning deliberations with Calhoun.

**75.** Washington, National Archives. Record Group 46: Records of the U.S. Senate, 28th and 29th Congresses. Reports of the secretary of state to Congress and accompanying documents.

Washington, National Archives. Record Group 59: General Records of the Department of State, in the following series:

**76.** Diplomatic Instructions. Letters from the secretary of state to U.S. ministers abroad. (Microcopy 77.)

**77.** Diplomatic Despatches. Reports from U.S. ministers abroad. See especially Great Britain (Microcopy 30); France (M-34); German States (M-44); China (M-92); Mexico (M-97); Brazil (M-121); Hawaii (Microcopy T-30); Colombia (T-33); Texas (T-728).

**78.** Notes to Foreign Legations. Letters to foreign ministers in Washington. (Microcopy 99.)

**79.** Notes from Foreign Legations. Letters from foreign ministers in Washington. Different microcopies by country. See especially Great Britain (M-50); France (M-53); Mexico (M-54); Spain (M-59); Texas (T-809).

**80.** Instructions to consular officers.

**81.** Consular Despatches. Reports from the many U.S. consuls and commercial agents abroad. Different Microcopies according to post.

**82.** Notes from foreign consuls in the U.S. (M-664.)

**83.** Domestic Letters. Letters to non-diplomatic correspondents. (M-40.)

**84.** Miscellaneous Letters. Letters from non-diplomatic correspondents. (M-179.)

**85.** Reports of the secretary of state to president and Congress.

**86.** Letters of Application and Recommendation During the Administrations of Martin Van Buren, William Henry Harrison, and John Tyler. (M-687.)

**87.** Washington, National Archives. Record Group 233: Records of the U.S. House of Representatives, 28th and 29th Congresses. Reports of the secretary of state to Congress, with accompanying documents.

## 7. As Senator, 1845–1850

**88.** Washington, National Archives. Record Group 46: Records of the U.S. Senate, 29th–31st Congresses. Bills, resolutions, committee reports, and other documents.

## D. PUBLISHED OFFICIAL PAPERS

### 1. As Secretary of War, 1817–1825

**89.** *American State Papers: Documents, Legislative and Executive, of the Congress* . . . . 37 vols. Washington: various printers, 1832–1861. Reports of the secretary of war to Congress, with accompanying documents, in the series "Military Affairs," and "Indian Affairs."

**90.** Carter, Clarence E., and John Porter Bloom, eds. *The Territorial Papers of the United States.* 28 vols. to date. Washington: U.S. Government Printing Office, 1934–. Calhoun materials, especially but not exclusively in the War Department period.

**91.** Harden, Edward J. *The Life of George M. Troup.* Savannah, Ga.: E.J. Purse, 1859. Five letters exchanged by Secretary of War Calhoun and the governor of Georgia over Indian matters.

**92.** U.S. House of Representatives, *Documents,* 15th–18th Congresses. Reports of the secretary of war to Congress, with accompanying documents.

**93.** U.S. Senate, *Documents,* 15th–18th Congresses. More of the same.

### 2. As Secretary of State, 1844–1845

**94.** Bourne, Kenneth, ed. *British Documents on Foreign Affairs. Reports and Papers from the Foreign Office Confidential Print.* Part One, Series C: *North America, 1838–1914.* 4 vols. Frederick, Md.: University Publications of America, 1986.

**95.** *British and Foreign State Papers.* 170 vols. London: HMSO, 1812–1968. Vols. 33 and 34 contain official British documents on American relations during Calhoun's tenure in the State Department.

**96.** *Correspondence Relative to the Negotiation of the Question of Disputed Right to the Oregon Territory, on the North-west Coast of America; Subsequent to the Treaty of Washington of August 9, 1842. Presented to Both Houses of Parliament by Command of Her Majesty, 1846.* London: T.R. Harrison, no date. The 1844–1845 negotiations between Calhoun and the British minister to the U.S., Richard Pakenham, over Oregon.

**97.** Davids, Jules, ed. *American Diplomatic and Public Papers: The United States and China,* Series I [1842–1860]. 2 vols. Wilmington, Del.: Scholarly Resources, Inc., 1973. Papers of the first U.S. mission to China, carried out and concluded in 1844 (facsimile edition).

**98.** Garrison, George P., ed. *Diplomatic Correspondence of the Republic of Texas.* In the *American Historical Association Annual Report* for 1907, vol. 2, and for 1908, vol. 2. Washington: U.S. Government Printing Office, 1908–1911.

**99.** Irving, Washington, *Letters.* Edited by Ralph M. Aderman et al. 4 vols. Boston: Twayne: 1978–1982 (comprising vols. 23–26 of *The Complete Works of Washington Irving*). Letters from Irving as U.S. Minister to Spain to Secretary of State Calhoun.

**100.** Larkin, Thomas O. *The Larkin Papers. Personal, Business, and Official Correspondence of Thomas Oliver Larkin, Merchant and United States Consul in California.* Edited by George P. Hammond. 11 vols. Berkeley Calif.: University of California Press, 1951–1968. The first U.S. representative in then Mexican California took office while Calhoun was secretary of state.

**101.** Manning, William R., ed. *Diplomatic Correspondence of the United States: Canadian Relations, 1784–1860.* 4 vols. Washington: Carnegie Endowment for International Peace, 1940–1945. Much official correspondence about the northeastern boundary and other matters.

**102.** ———. *Diplomatic Correspondence of the United States: Inter-American Affairs, 1831–1860.* 12 vols. Washington: Carnegie Endowment for International Peace, 1932–1939. Much material relating to relations with Central and South America.

**103.** U.S. House of Representatives, *Documents,* 28th and 29th Congresses. Reports of the secretary of state to Congress, with accompanying papers.

# Manuscript and Archival Resources

**104.** U.S. Senate, *Documents,* 28th and 29th Congresses. Reports of the secretary of state to Congress, with accompanying papers.

## E. UNPUBLISHED PAPERS OF ASSOCIATES

### 1. Major Collections

This category includes important associates or lieutenants of Calhoun whose papers contain not only correspondence with Calhoun but significant comment on him or record of activities carried on in his behalf.

Thomas Green Clemson (1807–1888). Scientist, diplomat, son-in-law of John C. Calhoun.

**105.** Clemson, S.C., Clemson University. Thomas Green Clemson Papers, 1833–1888. 1,000 items. Family papers which supplement #1.

Richard Kenner Crallé (1800–1864). Virginia journalist, chief clerk of the State Department when Calhoun was secretary of state, and editor of *The Works of John C. Calhoun.*

**106.** Charlottesville, Va., University of Virginia. Richard K. Crallé Papers, 1829–1860. *ca.* 200 items.

**107.** Washington, Library of Congress, Manuscripts Division. Richard K. Crallé Papers, 1814–1861 *ca.* 50 items. (See #29)

Franklin Harper Elmore (1799–1850). South Carolina banker, congressman, Calhoun's informal in-state political manager.

**108.** Chapel Hill, N.C., University of North Carolina, Southern Historical Collection. Franklin Harper Elmore Papers, 1819–1910. 110 items and 1 vol.

**109.** Washington, Library of Congress, Manuscripts Division. Franklin Harper Elmore Papers, 1795–1858. 1,750 items. (See #29)

Duff Green (1791–1875). Editor, entrepreneur, kinsman by marriage and long-time Calhoun political lieutenant.

**110.** Chapel Hill, N.C., University of North Carolina, Southern Historical Collection. Duff Green Papers, 1810–1902. 3,600 items and 29 vols. Massive collection reflecting Green's journalistic, political, entrepreneurial, and diplomatic activities on behalf of Calhoun and the Southern economy. Also papers of his son, Ben E. Green, author, Calhoun lieutenant, and acting U.S. chargé d'affaires in Mexico when Calhoun was secretary of state. (Published microfilm available.)

**111.** Washington, Library of Congress, Manuscripts Division. Duff Green Papers, 1813–1879. 1,200 items. More of the same. (See #29)


Robert Mercer Taliaferro Hunter (1809–1887). Speaker of U.S. House of Representatives, senator from Virginia, Calhoun intimate and congressional ally.

**112.** Charlottesville, Va., Univesity of Virginia. Robert M.T. Hunter Papers, 1826–1887. 2,700 items. (Published microfilm available.)

**113.** Richmond, Va., Virginia Historical Society. Hunter Family Papers, 1766–1918. 15 boxes.

**114.** Richmond, Va., Virginia State Library. Robert M.T. Hunter Papers, 1820–1876. 875 items.


Andrew Jackson (1767–1845). Major General in command of the Southern Department of the U.S. Army under Calhoun as secretary of war, political ally and later enemy, and president during Calhoun's second term as vice president.

**115.** Washington, Library of Congress, Manuscripts Division. Andrew Jackson Papers, 1775–1860. Extensive material to, from, and about Calhoun. (Presidential Papers Microfilm, 78 reels.)


Dixon Hall Lewis (1802–1848). Representative and senator from Alabama, Calhoun intimate and congressional ally.

**116.** Austin, Texas, University of Texas, Barker Texas History Center. Dixon H. Lewis Papers, 1833–1865. 1 ft.

# Manuscript and Archival Resources

Virgil Maxcy (1785–1844). Maryland planter and lawyer, Litchfield Law School classmate and lifelong close friend of Calhoun.

**117.** Washington, Library of Congress. Galloway-Maxcy-Markoe Papers, 1654–1888. 15,000 items. The portion of the collection relating to Virgil Maxcy contains many letters from Calhoun and extensive materials reflecting Maxcy's activities on Calhoun's behalf during both of his presidential campaigns and at other times. (See #29)

James Monroe (1758–1831). Calhoun was in close association with President Monroe for more than seven years, his chief while Calhoun was secretary of war, and remained on cordial terms for the rest of Monroe's life.

**118.** Washington, Library of Congress, Manuscripts Division. James Monroe Papers, 1758–1839. (Presidential Papers microfilm, 11 reels.)

## 2. Other Collections with Significant Materials

**119.** Boston, Massachusetts Historical Society. Adams Family Papers. John Quincy Adams's papers contain a great deal of material to, from, and about Calhoun, especially in his diary while they were colleagues in the Monroe cabinet. (Published microfilm available.)

**120.** Chapel Hill, N.C., University of North Carolina, Southern Historical Collection. William Lowndes Papers. Lowndes was a nationally known representative from S.C. and close colleague of Calhoun in his early career. (Published microfilm available.)

**121.** Chapel Hill, N.C., University of North Carolina, Southern Historical Collection. Robert Barnwell Rhett Papers. Only a few Calhoun items but some material about Calhoun; most of the collection is dated after Calhoun's death.

**122.** Columbia, S.C., University of South Carolina, South Caroliniana Library. James Edward Calhoun (Colhoun) Papers, 1806–1889. 597 items. Papers of Calhoun's brother-in-law and close friend.

**123.** Columbia, S.C., University of South Carolina, South Caroliniana Library. John Ewing Colhoun Papers, 1769–1822. 405 items. Papers of Calhoun's father-in-law and his family.

**124.** Columbia, S.C., University of South Carolina, South Caroliniana Library. Francis W. Pickens Papers. Some material in a small collection of a kinsman of Calhoun.

**125.** Columbia, S.C., University of South Carolina, South Caroliniana Library. James A. Seddon Manuscripts. Small collection of a Virginia political ally.

**126.** Columbia, S.C., University of South Carolina, South Caroliniana Library. Townes Family Papers. A family related to Calhoun by marriage.

**127.** Durham, N.C., Duke University. George McDuffie Papers, 1819–1870. 250 items. Small collection of papers of a Calhoun lieutenant.

**128.** Notre Dame, Ind., University of Notre Dame. Orestes A. Brownson Collection. Brownson was a Northern intellectual who was philosophically and actively involved with Calhoun during the early years of Brownson's career. (Published microfilm available.)

**129.** New York, New York Public Library. Samuel L. Gouverneur Papers. Series of Calhoun letters to James Monroe's son-in-law, 1823–1836.

**130.** New York, New York Public Library. James Monroe Papers. More than 20 Calhoun items.

**131.** Washington, Library of Congress, Manuscripts Division, Henry Clay Papers. Papers of the national leader of the Whig party whose career paralleled Calhoun's in association and rivalry. (Published microfilm available.)

**132.** Washington, Library of Congress, Manuscripts Division. James Henry Hammond Papers. Correspondence with Calhoun by a S.C. political leader and diaries which incorporate a running commentary on Calhoun. (Published microfilm available.)

**133.** Washington, Library of Congress, Manuscripts Division. James K. Polk Papers. Includes about a dozen Calhoun items and material about Calhoun. (Presidential Papers Microfilm.)

**134.** Washington, Library of Congress, Manuscripts Division. William Cabell Rives Papers. Large collection of a leading Virginia politician

# Manuscript and Archival Resources

often antagonistic to Calhoun.

**135.** Washington, Library of Congress, Manuscripts Division. John Tyler Papers. Relatively little material related directly to Calhoun in this small collection of papers of the president who appointed him secretary of state. (Presidential Papers Microfilm.)

**136.** Washington, Library of Congress, Manuscripts Division. Martin Van Buren Papers. Few Calhoun documents but a good deal of comment on Calhoun. (Presidential Papers Microfilm.)

## F. PUBLISHED PAPERS OF ASSOCIATES

### 1. Major Collections

**137.** Hunter, Robert M.T. *Correspondence of Robert M.T. Hunter, 1826–1876.* Edited by Charles Henry Ambler. In *American Historical Association Annual Report* for 1916, vol. 2. Washington: U.S. Government Printing Office, 1918. Political correspondence of Calhoun's most prominent supporter in Virginia.

**138.** Jackson, Andrew. *The Correspondence of Andrew Jackson.* Edited by John Spencer Bassett. 7 vols. Washington: Carnegie Institution of Washington, 1926–1935. Much Calhoun material.

**139.** ———. *Microfilm Edition of The Papers of Andrew Jackson.* Edited by Harold D. Moser and others. 39 reels. Wilmington. Del.: Scholarly Resources, 1986. An immense gathering of Jackson materials from sources other than the Library of Congress (#115) and National Archives.

**140.** Monroe, James. *The Writings of James Monroe, Including a Collection of His Public and Private Papers and Correspondence* . . . . Edited by Stanislaus M. Hamilton. 7 vols. New York: G.P. Putnam's Sons, 1898–1903. Much Calhoun material in the Monroe administration and afterward.

**141.** Moore, Frederick W., ed. "Calhoun as Seen by His Political Friends: Letters of Duff Green, Dixon H. Lewis [and] Richard K. Crallé During the Period from 1831 to 1848." *Publications of the Southern History Association* 7 (1903). Excerpts from letters exchanged by three of Calhoun's most intimate friends and supporters.

## 2. Other Publications with Significant Material

**142.** Adams, John Quincy. *Memoirs of John Quincy Adams, Comprising Portions of His Diary from 1795 to 1848.* Edited by Charles Francis Adams. 12 vols. Philadelphia: J.B. Lippincott, 1874–1877. Calhoun figures importantly in Adams's running private commentary on American events for many years.

**143.** Allston, Robert F.W. *The South Carolina Rice Plantation as Revealed in the Papers of Robert F.W. Allston.* Edited by J. Harold Easterby. Chicago: University of Chicago Press, 1945. Many mentions of Calhoun in the papers of an extended and articulate Low Country plantation family.

**144.** Biddle, Nicholas. *The Correspondence of Nicholas Biddle Dealing with National Affairs, 1807–1844.* Edited by Reginald C. McGrane. Boston and New York: Houghton Mifflin Co., 1919. Calhoun figures as both a correspondent and subject in the letters of the president of the Second Bank of the United States.

**145.** [Brownson, Orestes A.] *The Brownson-Hecker Correspondence.* Edited by Joseph F. Gower and Richard M. Leliart. South Bend, Ind.: University of Notre Dame Press, 1979. Letters between Brownson and Isaac T. Hecker, two young Northern intellectuals active in Calhoun's 1844 presidential campaign.

**146.** Buchanan, James. *The Works of James Buchanan.* Edited by John Bassett Moore. 12 vols. Philadelphia: J.B. Lippincott, 1908–1911. Buchanan's career paralleled Calhoun's, largely as associates and rivals in the Democratic party.

**147.** Clay, Henry. *The Papers of Henry Clay.* Edited by James F. Hopkins, Mary W.M. Hargreaves, and others. 9 vols. to date. Lexington, Ky.: University of Kentucky Press, 1959–.

**148.** ———. *Works of Henry Clay.* Edited by Calvin Colton. 6 vols. New York: A.S. Barnes & Co., 1857.

**149.** [Crawford, William H.] *Giant Days, or the Life and Times of William H. Crawford, Embracing Also Excerpts from His Diary, Letters and Speeches.* By J.E.D. Shipp. Americus, Ga.: Southern Printers, 1909. Calhoun's arch-rival.

## Manuscript and Archival Resources

**150.** Edwards, Ninian W. *History of Illinois, from 1778 to 1833; and Life and Times of Ninian Edwards.* Springfield, Ill.: Illinois State Journal Printing Co., 1870. Includes documents relating to Calhoun's relationship with the major political figure of early Illinois.

**151.** [Floyd, John.] *The Life and Diary of John Floyd, Governor of Virginia, an Apostle of Secession, and the Father of the Oregon Country.* By Charles Henry Ambler. Richmond, Va.: Richmond Press, Inc., 1918. Diary of the pro-Nullification governor of Virginia and other Calhoun-related material.

**152.** Hammond, James H. "Memorandum by James H. Hammond." *American Historical Review* 6 (July 1901): 741–745. An interview with Calhoun in 1831.

**153.** ———. *Secret and Sacred: The Diaries of James Henry Hammond.* Edited by Carol K. Bleser. New York: Oxford University Press, 1988. Hammond was a public defender and private critic of Calhoun.

**154.** Houston, Samuel. *The Writings of Sam Houston.* Edited by Amelia W. Williams and Eugene C. Barker. 8 vols. Austin, Texas: University of Texas Press, 1938–1941. Houston was Cherokee Indian Agent under Calhoun as secretary of war and the leading figure of the Texas Republic when Calhoun was secretary of state.

**155.** Hunter, Martha T. *A Memoir of Robert M.T. Hunter.* Washington: Neale Publishing Co., 1903. Incorporates original documents of Calhoun's Virginia lieutenant.

**156.** [Ingersoll, Charles J.] *The Life of Charles Jared Ingersoll.* By William M. Meigs. Philadelphia: J.B. Lippincott, 1900. Includes diary of the Philadelphia congressman who was well acquainted with Calhoun for many years and was chairman of the House Foreign Relations Committee.

**157.** Jackson, Andrew. *The Papers of Andrew Jackson.* Edited by Samuel B. Smith, Harold D. Moser and others. 2 vols. to date. Knoxville, Tenn.: University of Tennessee Press, 1980–. Projected selective edition.

**158.** Lincoln, Abraham. *The Collected Works of Abraham Lincoln.* Edited by Roy P. Basler. 8 vols. New Brunswick, N.J.: Rutgers University Press, 1953. Young Lincoln's support for Calhoun's public land policies (1:135–138, 181).

**159.** Madison, James. *The Papers of James Madison, Presidential Series.* Edited by William T. Hutchinson and others. 1 vol. to date. Chicago: University of Chicago Press, 1984–.

**160.** Monroe, James. *Microfilm Edition of James Monroe Papers in Virginia Repositories.* 13 reels. Charlottesville, Va.: University of Virginia Library, 1969.

**161.** Phillips, Ulrich B., ed. *The Correspondence of Robert Toombs, Alexander H. Stephens, and Howell Cobb.* In *American Historical Association Annual Report* for 1911, vol. 2. pp. 7–743. Washington: U.S. Government Printing Office, 1913. Extensive correspondence between the three leading figures of Georgia politics during the latter part of Calhoun's career.

**162.** Polk, James K. *The Correspondence of James K. Polk.* Edited by Herbert Weaver and E. Wayne Cutler. 6 vols. to date. Nashville, Tenn.: Vanderbilt University Press, 1969–.

**163.** ———. *Polk: The Diary of a President, 1845–1849.* Edited by Allan Nevins. 1929; reprint, New York: Capricorn Books, 1968. Senator Calhoun figures prominently in Polk's diary in struggles over Oregon and the Mexican War.

**164.** Ruffin, Edmund. *The Diary of Edmund Ruffin, 1856–1865.* Edited by William K. Scarborough. 3 vols. Baton Rouge, La.: Louisiana State University Press, 1972–1988. Although the great Southern fire-eater and agricultural reformer began his diary after Calhoun's death, he recorded several interesting recollections and comments upon Calhoun.

**165.** Simms, William Gilmore. *The Letters of William Gilmore Simms.* Edited by Mary C. Simms Oliphant, Alfred Taylor Odell, and T.C. Duncan Eaves. 6 vols. Columbia: University of South Carolina Press, 1952–1982. Occasional letters to and comments on Calhoun by South Carolina's leading literary figure.

**166.** Tyler, Lyon G., ed. *The Letters and Times of the Tylers.* 3 vols. Richmond, Va.: Whittet and Shepperson, 1884–1896. Calhoun's relations with President Tyler, his administration, and family.

**167.** Webster, Daniel. *Microfilm Edition of the Papers of Daniel Webster.* Edited by Charles M. Wiltse. 41 reels. Ann Arbor, Mich.: University Microfilms International, 1971.

## Manuscript and Archival Resources

**168.** ———. *The Papers of Daniel Webster. Series I. Correspondence*, 7 vols. *Series II. Legal Papers*, 3 vols. *Series III. Diplomatic Papers*, 2 vols. *Series IV. Speeches and Formal Writings*, 2 vols. Edited by Charles M. Wiltse and others. Hanover, N.H.: University Press of New England, 1974–1988.

### G. CONTEMPORARY NEWSPAPERS AND PERIODICALS

#### 1. Newspapers

**169.** Albany, N.Y., *Argus*, 1813–1856. Organ of the Van Buren organization. (Cornell University: microfilm available.)

**170.** Augusta, Ga., *States' Rights Sentinel*, 1834–1836. Pro-Calhoun paper edited by the author A. B. Longstreet. (Emory University.)

**171.** Auraria, Ga., *Western Herald*, 1833–1835. Weekly published in the gold mining region where Calhoun often visited. (University of Georgia: microfilm available.)

**172.** Baltimore, Md., *Pilot and Transcript*, 1840–1841. Paper edited by Duff Green during the election of 1840, when he differed with Calhoun and supported the Whigs. (Library of Congress.)

**173.** Boston *Post*, 1831–1956. An independent Democratic party paper sometimes friendly to Calhoun. (Library of Congress: microfilm available.)

**174.** Charleston, S.C., *Courier*, 1803–1852. Organ of the Charleston commercial community, less sympathetic to Calhoun than the *Mercury*. (South Caroliniana Library, University of South Carolina; Library of Congress: microfilm available.)

**175.** Charleston, S.C., *Mercury*, 1822–1868. The ably edited daily organ of the South Carolina states rights party. (Library of Congress; South Caroliniana Library, University of South Carolina: microfilm available.)

**176.** Columbia, S.C., *South-Carolinian*, 1838–1849? The major paper in the South Carolina capital in its time. (South Caroliniana Library, University of South Carolina: incomplete files.)

**177.** Columbia. S.C., *Southern Times and State Gazette,* 1830–1838? Pro-nullification paper in the South Carolina capital. (South Caroliniana Library, University of South Carolina: incomplete files.)

**178.** Columbia, S.C., *Telescope,* 1815——? Journal in the South Carolina capital. (Incomplete files, South Caroliniana Library, University of South Carolina.)

**179.** Edgefield, S.C., *Advertiser,* 1836–. A fire-eater organ. (South Caroliniana Library, University of South Carolina.)

**180.** Grand Rapids, Mich., *Enquirer,* 1841–1863. Supported Calhoun's presidential candidacy in 1843–1844. (Michigan State Library: microfilm available.)

**181.** Jackson, Miss., *Southern Reformer,* 1843–1846. Pro-Calhoun paper. (Mississippi Department of Archives: microfilm available.)

**182.** Lynchburg, Va., *Jeffersonian Republican,* 1828–1833. Pro-Calhoun newspaper edited by Richard K. Crallé. (University of Virginia: scattered files.)

**183.** New Orleans, La., *Jeffersonian Republican,* 1844–1845. Pro-Calhoun and pro-Texas annexation newspaper in the metropolis of the West. (Library of Congress.)

**184.** New York *Democratic Republican New Era,* 1840–1842. Organ of radical New York Democrats often sympathetic to Calhoun. (Library of Congress.)

**185.** New York *Evening Post,* 1832–1920. Organ of Free Soil Democrats. (Widely available: microfilm available.)

**186.** New York *Gazette,* 1843. Supported Calhoun's presidential candidacy. (No significant files survive.)

**187.** New York *Herald,* 1835–1924. A pioneering mass-circulation and human-interest paper with colorful commentary on public figures. (Widely available: microfilm available.)

**188.** New York *Journal of Commerce,* 1827–1892? Organ of commercial free trade interests. (Harvard University: microfilm available.)

**189.** New York *Republic,* 1844–1845. Pro-Calhoun newspaper edited by Duff Green. (No significant files survive.)

# Manuscript and Archival Resources

**190.** Pendleton, S.C., *Messenger*, 1807–? Weekly published in the neighborhood where Calhoun lived from 1826 to 1850. (South Caroliniana Library, University of South Carolina.)

**191.** Petersburg, Va. *Republican*, 1843–1850. One of several efforts to provide a Calhoun organ for Virginia in opposition to the Richmond *Enquirer*. (Virginia State Library.)

**192.** Portsmouth, Va., *Old Dominion*, 1838–1846. One of several examples of pro-Calhoun newspapers in Virginia attempting to counter the Richmond *Enquirer*. (Library of Congress.)

**193.** Richmond, Va., *Enquirer*, 1804–1877. Guiding organ of Southern Democrats who did not follow Calhoun. (Library of Congress; University of Virginia: microfilm available.)

**194.** St. Clairsville, Ohio, *Gazette*, 1824–. The best of several examples of Midwestern newspapers supportive of Calhoun's politics. (Ohio Historical Society: microfilm available.)

**195.** Washington and Philadelphia *Banner of the Constitution*, 1829–1833. Pro-Nullification paper ably edited by Philadelphia free trader Condy Raguet. (University of South Carolina.)

**196.** Washington *Chronicle*, 1838–1839. Short-lived organ of Calhoun supporters. (Library of Congress.)

**197.** Washington *Constitution*, 1844–1845. Organ of Calhoun supporters. (Library of Congress.)

**198.** Washington *Daily National Intelligencer*, 1800–1870. Organ of the hostile Whig party during most of Calhoun's career. (Library of Congress: microfilm available.)

**199.** Washington *Globe*, 1830–1845. Organ of Jackson-Van Buren Democrats during Calhoun's central period. (Library of Congress: microfilm available.)

**200.** Washington *Madisonian*, 1837–1845. Organ of the Tyler administration while Calhoun was an administration supporter in the Senate and in the cabinet. (Library of Congress: microfilm available.)

**201.** Washington *Reformer*, 1837. Short-lived organ of Calhoun supporters during a period independent of both Democratic and Whig parties. (Library of Congress.)

**202.** Washington *Republican and Congressional Examiner*, 1822–1824. Edited by Thomas L. McKenney in behalf of Calhoun's presidential candidacy. (Library of Congress.)

**203.** Washington *Spectator*, 1842–1844. Perhaps the most successful of several short-lived pro-Calhoun newspapers in the capital city. (Library of Congress.)

**204.** Washington *Union*, 1845–1859. National organ of Southern politics during last years of Calhoun's life. (Library of Congress: microfilm available.)

**205.** Washington *United States' Telegraph*, 1826–1837. Vigorous political daily edited by Duff Green, Calhoun's kinsman and ally. (Library of Congress: microfilm available.)

## 2. Periodicals

**206.** *Boston Quarterly Review.* Boston: 1838–1842. Edited by Orestes A. Brownson in his Calhoun period. (American Periodicals Series microfilm.)

**207.** *Brownson's Quarterly Review.* New York: 1844–1864. Pro-Calhoun in early period. (American Periodicals Series microfilm.)

**208.** *De Bow's Review.* New Orleans: 1846–1850. Organ of Southern political and economic nationalism during Calhoun's last years. (American Periodicals Series microfilm.)

**209.** *The Examiner, and Journal of Political Economy.* Philadelphia: 1833–1835. Lively free trade and pro-Nullification journal edited by Condy Raguet. (University of South Carolina.)

**210.** *Free Trade Advocate and Journal of Political Economy.* Philadelphia: 1829. Another Condy Raguet journal. (University of South Carolina.)

**211.** *Niles' Weekly Register.* Baltimore: 1811–1849. Excellent compendium of the major public documents and speeches of all parties, with even-handed reportage. (Widely available.)

## Manuscript and Archival Resources

**212.** *The Political Register.* Washington: 1832–1835. News magazine edited by Duff Green. (University of South Carolina.)

**213.** *The Subterranean and Working Man's Advocate.* New York: 1844–1847. Lively journal of the radical New York Democrats, often sympathetic to Calhoun. (American Periodicals Series microfilm.)

**214.** *United States Democratic Review.* Washington and New York: 1837–1859. Good for sorting out the various factions and perspectives as well as the unifying factors in the Democratic party. (American Periodicals Series microfilm.)

# II.
# Speeches and Writings of John C. Calhoun

### A. COLLECTIONS

See also *The Papers of John C. Calhoun* (#30).

**215.** *Calhoun: Basic Documents.* Edited by John M. Anderson. State College, Pa.: Bald Eagle Press, 1952. A small but well-selected collection of speeches and writings from all parts of Calhoun's career.

**216.** *Escritos de John C. Calhoun.* Translated by Juan Ignacio de Armas. 4 vols. Caracas: Imprenta de la Gaceta Official, 1879. Latin American edition (partial) of Crallé's *Works of John C. Calhoun*.

*The Works of John C. Calhoun.* Edited by Richard K. Crallé. 6 vols. Made up of:

**217.** Volume 1. *A Disquisition on Government* and *A Discourse on the Constitution and Government of the United States.* Columbia, S.C.: A.S. Johnston, 1851. The first publication (posthumous) and earliest known texts of Calhoun's two systematic treatises.

**218.** Volumes 2, 3, 4. *Speeches of John C. Calhoun, Delivered in the House of Representatives, and in the Senate of the United States.* New York: D. Appleton & Co., 1853, 1857. Collection of Calhoun's most important speeches in the House of Representatives, 1811–1817, and in the Senate, 1837–1843 and 1846–1850.

**219.** Volumes 5 and 6. *Reports and Public Letters of John C. Calhoun.* New York: D. Appleton & Co., 1857. Collection of Calhoun's official reports as secretary of war, important diplomatic correspondence as secretary of state, committee reports as senator, public letters on political subjects, shorter writings, and other documents.

(*The Works of John C. Calhoun* was reissued by Appleton in 1883 and possibly at other times in a stereotype reprint, and Volume 1 was also issued separately on several occasions in the same way.)

## B. SPEECHES

### 1. Collections

See also #30, #215, #218.

**220.** Briggs, Lillian M., ed. *Noted Speeches of Daniel Webster, Henry Clay, John C. Calhoun.* New York: Moffat, Yard & Co., 1912. A few major speeches reprinted from standard sources.

**221.** [Calhoun, John C., ed.] *Speeches of John C. Calhoun. Delivered in the Congress of the United States from 1811 to the Present Time.* New York: Harper & Brothers, 1843. Calhoun's major speeches in the Senate during 1833–1843, with a few other important documents.

**222.** Williston, Ebenezer B., ed. *Eloquence of the United States.* 5 vols. New York: Jonathan Seymour, 1830. Some early Calhoun speeches.

### 2. Compilations of Congressional Debates

These compilations contain not only the major speeches of Calhoun and other notables for the periods they cover, but also an account of the proceedings of both houses of Congress and reports of many lesser speeches and remarks in debate that do not appear in the major collections of individual statesmen.

**223.** *Abridgment of the Debates of Congress, from 1789 to 1850 . . . .* Edited by Thomas H. Benton. 16 vols. New York: D. Appleton & Co., 1854–1861. Sometimes artfully selected and arranged highlights from earlier collections.

**224.** *Annals of the Congress of the United States. Debates and Proceedings . . . 1791 . . . 1824.* 42 vols. Washington: Gales & Seaton, 1834–1856. Covers Calhoun in the House, 1811–1817.

**225.** *Congressional Globe . . . 1833–1873 . . . .* 46 vols. Washington: Blair & Rives and others, 1834–1873. Covers Calhoun in the Senate.

**226.** *The Register of Debates; Being a Report of the Speeches Delivered in the Two Houses of Congress, Reported for the United States Telegraph.* 4 vols. Washington: Duff Green, 1834–1835. Sometimes variant and additional accounts of Calhoun in the Senate for the period covered.

**227.** *Register of Debates in Congress . . . .* 14 vols. Washington: Gales & Seaton, 1825–1837. Covers Calhoun as vice president and his early years in the Senate.

### 3. Major Speeches

Calhoun's speeches constitute the most important part of his record. Even more than the few treatises, they contain the historical and philosophical commentary on the current and future state of the American Union which make him an important figure. His major speeches were published countless times: contemporaneously in newspapers, compilations of congressional debates, and one or more pamphlet versions; later in the various collections of his works and in anthologies of oratory and political thought. Through the year 1844, the speeches are cited below to *The Papers of John C. Calhoun* (#30), a fairly available modern source which contains a complete text, a publication history, and a discussion of variant versions for each. Speeches of 1845–1850 are located in *The Works of John C. Calhoun* (#218), edited by Richard K. Crallé. The titles given to the speeches are somewhat arbitrary and accidental conventions and vary considerably in the early sources. Titles given below are merely convenient descriptive labels. Several hundred additional lesser speeches and remarks in debate appear in the reports of congressional debates and in *The Papers of John C. Calhoun* that are not included here. It should be added that very few significant manuscript versions of Calhoun's speeches exist.

*a. In the U.S. House of Representatives, 1811–1817*

**228.** On Relations with Great Britain, December 12, 1811. *The Papers of John C. Calhoun,* 1:75–86. The young "War Hawk" takes on John Randolph of Roanoke.

**229.** On a Petition for the Repeal of the Embargo, May 6, 1812. *The Papers of John C. Calhoun,* 1:102–108. The necessity for resistance to Great Britain.

**230.** On the Proposed Suspension of Non-Importation, June 24, 1812. *The Papers of John C. Calhoun,* 1:126–135. Failure of the restrictive system to secure redress from European powers.

**231.** On the Merchants' Bonds, December 8, 1812. *The Papers of John C. Calhoun,* 1:136–146. On financing the war and the nature of patriotism.

**232.** On the Bill for an Additional Military Force, January 14, 1813. *The Papers of John C. Calhoun,* 1:150–162. Support of the war effort.

**233.** On the Dangers of Factious Opposition, January 15, 1814. *The Papers of John C. Calhoun,* 1:189–201. On patriotism and the justice of the war.

**234.** On the Loan Bill, February 25, 1814. *The Papers of John C. Calhoun,* 1:208–240. Further call to patriotism and the justice of the war.

**235.** On the Bill to Repeal the Embargo and Non-Importation Acts, April 6, 1814. *The Papers of John C. Calhoun,* 1:243–248. A plea for postwar free trade.

**236.** On the Military Situation, October 25, 1814. *The Papers of John C. Calhoun,* 1:254–259. Necessity to maintain the war effort.

**237.** On the Results of the War, February 27, 1815. *The Papers of John C. Calhoun,* 1:279–283. The vindication of American rights.

**238.** On the Commercial Treaty with Great Britain, January 9, 1816. *The Papers of John C. Calhoun,* 1:304–314. On the treaty-making power under the Constitution.

**239.** On the Revenue Bill, January 31, 1816. *The Papers of John C. Calhoun,* 1:316–331. The necessity of maintaining postwar defense.

**240.** On Introducing the National Bank Bill, February 26, 1816. *The Papers of John C. Calhoun,* 1:331–339. For a national bank and the resumption of a specie-based currency.

**241.** On the Tariff Bill, April 4, 1816. *The Papers of John C. Calhoun,* 1:347–357. Acceptance of a moderate and temporary postwar protective tariff.

**242.** On the Compensation Bill, January 17, 1817. *The Papers of John C. Calhoun,* 1:382–393. On the pay of Congress and the instruction of representatives.

**243.** On Internal Improvements, February 4, 1817. *The Papers of John C. Calhoun,* 1:398–409. The need to knit the Union together with comprehensive internal improvements, to be paid for by non-tax revenue.

*b. In the U.S. Senate, 1833–1843*

**244.** On the Nature and Power of the Federal Government, January 22, 1833. *The Papers of John C. Calhoun,* 12:18–26. The constitutional issues raised by nullification.

**245.** On the Force Bill, February 15 and 16, 1833. *The Papers of John C. Calhoun,* 12:45–94. Eloquent and dramatic exposition of state rights and the South Carolina position in the present crisis.

**246.** In Reply to Daniel Webster on the Force Bill, February 26, 1833. *The Papers of John C. Calhoun,* 12:101–137. The Union as a compact.

**247.** On the Removal of the Deposits, January 13, 1834. *The Papers of John C. Calhoun,* 12:200–225. The usurpation, irresponsibility, and corruption of the Jackson administration's attack on the national bank.

**248.** On the Bill to Continue the Charter of the National Bank, March 21, 1834. *The Papers of John C. Calhoun,* 12:247–271. Differentiates himself from the Whig support for the national bank and suggests other measures to meet the currency problem.

**249.** In Support of the Repeal of the Force Act, April 9, 1834. *The Papers of John C. Calhoun,* 12:277–298. The need to erase a dangerous precedent.

**250.** On the President's Protest, May 6, 1834. *The Papers of John C. Calhoun,* 12:302–318. Refutation of Jackson's protest against the Senate's censure.

**251.** On the Executive Patronage in Reply to Thomas H. Benton, February 13, 1835. *The Papers of John C. Calhoun,* 12:458–478. The need for reform of Jacksonian spoilsmanship.

**252.** On the President's Power of Removal from Office, February 20, 1835. *The Papers of John C. Calhoun,* 12:483–499. Need for reform of the executive removal power.

**253.** On the President's Message on Relations with France, January 18, 1836. *The Papers of John C. Calhoun,* 13:33–41. Against Jacksonian jingoism.

**254.** On Abolition Petitions, March 9, 1836. *The Papers of John C. Calhoun,* 13:91–110. Calhoun begins to respond to attacks on Southern slavery.

**255.** On His Bill to Prohibit the Circulation of Incendiary Publications through the Mail, April 12, 1836. *The Papers of John C. Calhoun,* 13:147–166. The Post Office should recognize state laws.

**256.** On His Bill to Regulate the Deposits of Public Money, May 28, 1836. *The Papers of John C. Calhoun,* 13:202–229. Proposals to correct the corruption and damage to the currency inflicted by the Jackson "pet bank" system.

**257.** On the Bill for the Admission of Michigan, January 2 and January 5, 1837. *The Papers of John C. Calhoun,* 13:329–352. Exploring questions of sovereignty and territory.

**258.** On Abolition Petitions, February 6, 1837. *The Papers of John C. Calhoun,* 13:387–398. Defense of slavery.

**259.** On His Bill to Cede the Unsold Public Lands to the Western States, February 9, 1837. *The Papers of John C. Calhoun,* 13:407–419. Proposals in regard to public lands and revenue to benefit the West.

**260.** On the Bill to Reduce the Tariff Duties on Certain Imports, February 23, 1837. *The Papers of John C. Calhoun,* 13:454–467. Exposing Whig attempts to circumvent the Compromise of 1833.

**261.** On the Bill Authorizing an Issue of Treasury Notes, September 18, 1837. *The Papers of John C. Calhoun,* 13:546–572. Opposes both the Whig national bank and the Democratic state bank system: Congress should take direct responsibility for the currency.

**262.** On His Amendment to Separate the Government and the Banks, October 3, 1837. *The Papers of John C. Calhoun,* 13:592–616. Proposal to separate the government and currency from control by the banking system.

**263.** On the Subtreasury Bill, February 15, 1838. *The Papers of John C. Calhoun,* 14:124–155. Defends the Van Buren administration Subtreasury as the best solution to the currency crisis.

**264.** In Reply to Henry Clay on the Subtreasury Bill, March 10, 1838. *The Papers of John C. Calhoun,* 14:163–199. He did not abandon the Whig party on banking questions because he never belonged to it.

**265.** In Reply to Daniel Webster on the Subtreasury Bill, March 22, 1838. *The Papers of John C. Calhoun,* 14:200–242. On currency and banking.

**266.** Against the Amended Subtreasury Bill, March 24, 1838. *The Papers of John C. Calhoun,* 14:243–248. Rejects the Subtreasury without his specie amendment.

**267.** On the Bill to Graduate the Price of Public Lands, January 16, 1839. *The Papers of John C. Calhoun,* 14:514–526. Constructive proposals for the West.

**268.** On the Bill to Prevent the Interference of Certain Federal Officers in Elections, February 22, 1839. *The Papers of John C. Calhoun,* 14:560–576. History of the struggle to prevent the consolidation of the Union.

**269.** On the Assumption of State Debts, February 5, 1840. *The Papers of John C. Calhoun,* 15:70–94. Unconstitutionality and inexpediency of the proposed federal assumption of state debts.

**270.** On the Case of the Brig Enterprise, March 13, 1840. *The Papers of John C. Calhoun,* 15:139–157. Demand for an end to British interference with American coastal ships with slaves on board.

**271.** On the Bankruptcy Bill, June 2, 1840. *The Papers of John C. Calhoun,* 15:246–265. Against the bailout of corporations by a federal bankruptcy act.

**272.** On the Preemption Bill, January 12, 1841. *The Papers of John C. Calhoun,* 15:423–444. Outlining a position on the public lands.

**273.** On John J. Crittenden's Distribution Bill, January 23, 1841. *The Papers of John C. Calhoun,* 15:449–466. The unconstitutionality and inexpediency of the Whig efforts to dissipate the revenue of the public lands.

**274.** In Reply to Webster and Clay on the Distribution Bill, January 30, 1841. *The Papers of John C. Calhoun,* 15:476–496. Continuation of the preceding debate.

**275.** On the Case of Alexander McLeod, June 11, 1841. *The Papers of John C. Calhoun,* 15:563–571. Against federal interference with state courts on the grounds of foreign relations.

**276.** On the Report of the Secretary of the Treasury, June 21, 1841. *The Papers of John C. Calhoun,* 15:577–591. On public revenue and debt.

**277.** On the Loan Bill, July 19, 1841. *The Papers of John C. Calhoun,* 15:630–640. Against the Whig program to increase the national debt.

**278.** On the Distribution Bill, August 24, 1841. *The Papers of John C. Calhoun,* 15:714–737. Continued war against the Whig effort to squander the public land revenue.

**279.** On the Treasury Note Bill, January 22, 1842. *The Papers of John C. Calhoun,* 16:58–81. On the public revenue and expenditures.

**280.** On the Veto Power, February 28, 1842. *The Papers of John C. Calhoun,* 16:135–155. Defence of John Tyler and exploration of the nature of the Union and of presidential power.

**281.** On Henry Clay's Resolutions on Revenues and Expenditures, March 16, 1842. *The Papers of John C. Calhoun,* 16:169–199. Against the Whig legislative program for centralization and support of vested interests.

**282.** On the Loan Bill, April 12, 1842. *The Papers of John C. Calhoun,* 16:220–233. More of the same.

**283.** On the Tariff Bill, August 5, 1842. *The Papers of John C. Calhoun,* 16:352–375. For free trade and against the tariff of 1842 as a betrayal of the Compromise of 1833.

**284.** On the Treaty of Washington, August 19, 1842. *The Papers of John C. Calhoun,* 16:393–410. In defense of Webster's treaty and an amicable settlement with Great Britain of the northeastern boundary.

**285.** On the Bill for the Occupation and Settlement of the Territory of Oregon, January 31, 1843. *The Papers of John C. Calhoun,* 16:638–653. Against provocation and for peace: American objectives can all be obtained by waiting—"masterful neglect."

*c. In the U.S. Senate, 1846–1850*

**286.** On the Resolutions for Abrogation of the Joint Occupancy of Oregon, March 16, 1846. *The Works of John C. Calhoun,* 4:258–290. A plea for peace and reason.

**287.** On the Army Pay Bill, May 14, 1846. *The Works of John C. Calhoun,* 4:290–303. Against the spoils system.

**288.** On the War Appropriation Bill, February 9, 1847. *The Works of John C. Calhoun,* 4:303–327. For limited war aims.

**289.** In Reply to Hopkins L. Turney of Tennessee, February 12, 1847. *The Works of John C. Calhoun,* 4:328–339. His position on the Mexican War.

**290.** On His Resolutions on the Slave Question, February 19, 1847. *The Works of John C. Calhoun,* 4:339–349. Equal rights of the South in the territories.

**291.** On the Slave Question, February 20, 1847. *The Works of John C. Calhoun,* 4:349–361. Review of the relations of North and South

**292.** In Reply to Thomas H. Benton, February 24, 1847. *The Works of John C. Calhoun,* 4:362–382. Position on the Mexican War.

**293.** On the War with Mexico, January 4, 1848. *The Works of John C. Calhoun,* 4:396–424. Against excessive territorial aspirations.

**294.** On the Ten Regiment Bill, March 16 and 17, 1848. *The Works of John C. Calhoun,* 4:425–450. On presidential power.

**295.** On the Resolutions Congratulating the French Nation on Their Revolution, March 30, 1848. *The Works of John C. Calhoun,* 4:450–454. Distinction between American republicanism and European revolution.

**296.** On the Proposed Occupation of Yucatan, May 15, 1848. *The Works of John C. Calhoun,* 4:454–479. Dangers to the Union and the Constitution from imperialism.

**297.** On the Oregon Bill, June 27, 1848. *The Works of John C. Calhoun,* 4:479–512. The rights of the South in the territories.

**298.** On the Bill to Extend the Missouri Compromise Line, August 12, 1849. *The Works of John C. Calhoun,* 4:513–535. Not a real solution to the sectional conflict.

**299.** On the Slavery Question, March 4, 1850. *The Works of John C. Calhoun,* 4:542–573. Against the compromise and a plea for the North to accept the burdens as well as the benefits of the Union: the compromise does not solve but postpones the crisis. Calhoun's last major speech, which had to be read by another senator.

*d. Other Speeches (Selected)*

**300.** On the Democratic-Republican Vice-Presidential Nomination, Columbia, S.C., 1808. *The Papers of John C. Calhoun,* 17:10–11. First political speech for which any record survives.

**301.** At Abbeville, S.C., May 27, 1825. *The Papers of John C. Calhoun,* 10:21–24. Affirmation of self-government of the people.

**302.** On the Powers of the Vice-President, in the Senate, April 15, 1826. *The Papers of John C. Calhoun,* 10:88–90. Defends his restraint in shutting off debate.

**303.** At Pendleton, S.C., September 7, 1826. *The Papers of John C. Calhoun,* 10:199–203. Relations of the vice president with the Adams administration.

**304.** At Charleston, S.C., November 22, 1833. *The Papers of John C. Calhoun,* 12:180–183. Reviewing the crisis through which the state has recently passed.

**305.** At Pendleton, S.C., August 12, 1836. *The Papers of John C. Calhoun,* 13:266–276. Review of the state of the country.

**306.** At Montgomery, Ala., May 8, 1841. *The Papers of John C. Calhoun,* 15:536–542. The need to defend the Jeffersonian system and defeat the Hamiltonian.

**307.** On Taking the Chair of the Memphis Convention, November 13, 1845. *The Works of John C. Calhoun,* 6:273–284. The economic development of the West.

**308.** At Charleston, March 9, 1847. *The Works of John C. Calhoun,* 4:382–396. Rights of the South under the Constitution.

## C. WRITINGS

### 1. Treatises

*a. The South Carolina Exposition,* 1828. On the unconstitutionality and injustice of the protective tariff and its last remaining remedy—state interposition.

**309.** "The South Carolina Exposition." In *The Papers of John C. Calhoun,* 10:442–553. This version includes texts of both Calhoun's draft of November 1828, and the somewhat different version published by the South Carolina legislature in December. Also a publishing history.

**310.** South Carolina General Assembly. *Exposition and Protest. Reported by the Special Committee of the House of Representatives, on the Tariff; Read and Ordered to be Printed, December 19th, 1828.* Columbia, S.C.: D.W. Sims, State Printer, 1829. The official version for distribution.

*b. A Disquisition on Government.* Calhoun's final philosophical statement, completed in the last weeks of his life and posthumously published.

**311.** *A Disquisition on Government.* In *The Works of John C. Calhoun,* edited by Richard K. Crallé (# 217), 1:1–107. This publication was the original and only text, upon which all subsequent publications have been based. No manuscript exists. The *Disquisition* has been occasionally reprinted, and excerpts from it have been printed in numerous places. Two well-known reprints are:

**312.** *A Disquisition on Government.* Edited by Naphtaly Levy. New York: Political Science Classics, 1947. A facsimile reprint of the text of the *Disquisition* with a new title page.

**313.** Post, C. Gordon, ed. *Calhoun: A Disquisition on Government and Selections from the Discourse.* Indianapolis: Bobbs-Merrill Educational Publishing, 1953 (and later editions). Widely available edition of the text of Calhoun's most important writing.

*c. A Discourse on the Constitution and Government of the United States.* Calhoun's review of the history of the American Constitution. Probably unfinished.

**314.** *A Discourse on the Constitution and Government of the United States.* In *The Works of John C. Calhoun,* edited by Richard K. Crallé (# 217), 1:111–406. The first and only text. No manuscript exists. The *Discourse* has never been separately printed, except in excerpts.

**2. Official Reports (Selected)**

Official reports—written for a committee as a member of Congress or as a report to Congress when a member of the executive branch—constitute a significant part of Calhoun's writings and public career. They are what in more recent times would be called "position papers." As with speeches, such documents exist in some combination of multiple versions: archival manuscripts, printed congressional documents, the early collections of Calhoun's works, and others. Whenever possible, these documents are cited below to *The Papers of John C. Calhoun*

(# 30), where there is a definitive text and an accounting of extant versions; otherwise to an early authentic source. The titles supplied are merely arbitrary and convenient descriptive labels. In their early form many such documents had variant titles or none—they might come into existence in the form of a letter from the secretary of war to the speaker of the House of Representatives, for instance. The dates used are those of the actual reports. In some published versions a different and later date is used, representing the date on which the document was transmitted to Congress.

*a. In the U.S. House of Representatives, 1811–1817*

**315.** On Relations with Great Britain, November 29, 1811. *The Papers of John C. Calhoun,* 1:63–71. For the Foreign Relations Committee, on the causes for American complaint against the great power.

**316.** On the Causes and Reasons for the War, June 3, 1812. *The Papers of John C. Calhoun,* 1:109–125. For the Foreign Relations Committee, in justification of a declaration of war against Great Britain.

**317.** On Presenting the Bill for the Repeal of the Embargo and Non-Importation Acts, April 4, 1814. *The Papers of John C. Calhoun,* 1:240–243. For the Committee on Foreign Relations, to repeal the harmful and ineffective prewar system of trade restriction.

**318.** On Presenting a Bill to Incorporate a Bank of the United States, January 8, 1816. *The Papers of John C. Calhoun,* 1:290–304. For the Select Committee on Currency: Calhoun's plan for a national bank and sound currency.

*b. As Secretary of War, 1817–1825*

**319.** On the System of Indian Trade, December 5, 1818. *The Papers of John C. Calhoun,* 3:341–355. Recommendations to the House of Representatives.

**320.** On the Reduction of the Army, December 11, 1818. *The Papers of John C. Calhoun,* 3:374–386. To the House of Representatives, plans for coping with postwar retrenchment.

**321.** On Roads and Canals, January 7, 1819. *The Papers of John C. Calhoun,* 3:461–473. A plan of internal improvements, as requested by the House of Representatives.

**322.** On an Additional Military Academy, January 15, 1819. *The Papers of John C. Calhoun,* 3:495–497. To a House committee, recommending a second military academy in the West.

**323.** On the Yellow Stone Expedition, December 29, 1819. *The Papers of John C. Calhoun,* 4:519–524. To a House committee: plans for a western exploring expedition.

**324.** On the Civilization of the Indians, January 15, 1820. *The Papers of John C. Calhoun,* 4:575–577. Recommendations to the House of Representatives for reform and more humane efforts.

**325.** On the Military Academy, February 23, 1820. *The Works of John C. Calhoun,* 5:72–80. To the House of Representatives: recommendations for better organization.

**326.** On the Reduction of the Army, December 12, 1820. *The Papers of John C. Calhoun,* 5:480–491. To the House of Representatives: plans for a small but efficient and expansible standing army.

**327.** On Expenditures for the Civilization of the Indians, January 19, 1822. *The Works of John C. Calhoun,* 5:99–103. Recommendations to the president.

**328.** On the Condition of the Several Indian Tribes, February 8, 1822. *The Papers of John C. Calhoun,* 6:679–683. Recommendations to the president on provisions for education.

**329.** On the Accountability of Agents, February 11, 1822. *The Papers of John C. Calhoun,* 6:686–688. Recommendations to a House committee.

**330.** On the Condition of the Military Establishments and Fortifications, November 27, 1822. *The Papers of John C. Calhoun,* 7:356–358. Report to the president on the reductions in expenditure and improvements in accountability and efficiency in the Army.

**331.** On the Condition of the Military Establishment, Fortifications, and Militia, November 29, 1823. *The Papers of John C. Calhoun,* 8:384–387. Report to the president.

**332.** On the Condition of the Military Establishment and Fortifications, December 3, 1824. *The Papers of John C. Calhoun,* 9:421–429. On activities in various branches of the Army, including internal improvements surveys by the Engineers.

*c. In the U.S. Senate, 1833–1843*

**333.** Report of the Select Committee on the Extent of the Executive Patronage, February 9, 1835. *The Papers of John C. Calhoun,* 12:415–497. Calhoun's indictment of Jacksonian spoilsmanship and recommendations of reform legislation.

**334.** Report of the Select Committee on the Circulation of Incendiary Publications, February 4, 1836. *The Papers of John C. Calhoun,* 13:53–69. Calhoun's position on the duties and powers of the federal government in regard to abolitionism.

**335.** Report on the Bill to Cede the Public Lands to the Western States, May 13, 1840. *The Papers of John C. Calhoun,* 15:208–228. A report made by Senator John Norvell of Michigan but written by Calhoun: an attempt to settle the larger questions related to public lands, revenue, and internal improvements.

*d. As Secretary of State, 1844–1845*

**336.** To Richard Pakenham, British Minister to the U.S., April 18, 1844. *The Papers of John C. Calhoun,* 18:273–278. Reasons for the annexation of Texas.

**337.** To President John Tyler, May 16, 1844. *The Papers of John C. Calhoun,* 18:526–527. Probable course of Texas if annexation fails.

**338.** To Henry A. Wise, May 25, 1844. *The Papers of John C. Calhoun,* 18:621–624. Instructions as U.S. minister to Brazil.

**339.** To William Crump, May 28, 1844. *The Papers of John C. Calhoun,* 18:637–640. Instructions as U.S. minister to Chile.

**340.** To Tilghman A. Howard, June 18, 1844. *The Papers of John C. Calhoun,* 19:117–120. Instructions as U.S. minister to Texas.

**341.** To Wilson Shannon, June 20, 1844. *The Papers of John C. Calhoun,* 19:136–142. Instructions as U.S. minister to Mexico.

**342.** To Henry Wheaton, June 28, 1844. *The Papers of John C. Calhoun,* 19:208–212. Instructions as U.S. minister to Prussia.

**343.** To Edward Everett, U.S. Minister to Great Britain, August 7, 1844. *The Papers of John C. Calhoun,* 19:528–535. On the return of fugitive slaves under the Treaty of 1842.

**344.** To William R. King, U.S. Minister to France, August 12, 1844. *The Papers of John C. Calhoun,* 19:568–578. On presenting the annexation of Texas to European governments and the imperial interests behind the philanthropy of British antislavery.

**345.** To Richard Pakenham, September 3, 1844. *The Papers of John C. Calhoun,* 19:695–705. The American claims to Oregon.

**346.** To Wilson Shannon, September 10, 1844. *The Papers of John C. Calhoun,* 19:743–750. On U.S. relations with Mexico.

**347.** To Richard Pakenham, September 20, 1844. *The Papers of John C. Calhoun,* 19:814–819. Further on the American claims to Oregon.

**348.** To Edward Everett, September 25, 1844. *The Papers of John C. Calhoun,* 19:848–852. Further on Great Britain and the return of fugitive slaves.

**349.** On Alleged Errors in the Sixth Census, February 8, 1845. *The Works of John C. Calhoun,* 5:458–461. On the depressed condition of the freed blacks in the North.

**350.** To Andrew J. Donelson, U.S. Minister to Texas, March 3, 1845. *The Works of John C. Calhoun,* 5:393–399. Means of effecting annexation.

*e. In the U.S. Senate, 1845–1850*

**351.** Report from the Select Committee on the Memphis Memorial, June 26, 1846. *The Works of John C. Calhoun,* 5:246–311. On the internal improvements power and the development of the Mississippi Valley.

## 3. Essays, Articles, and Unofficial Reports

**352.** Resolutions on the Chesapeake-Leopard Affair, Abbeville, S.C., August 3, 1807. *The Papers of John C. Calhoun,* 1:34–37. First notable public effort.

**353.** "Onslow" [John C. Calhoun] to the Washington National Journal, May 20, 1826. *The Papers of John C. Calhoun,* 10:99–104. Predecessor to next item, not included in pamphlet publication.

**354.** "Onslow" to "Patrick Henry," June 27 and June 29, 1826. *The Papers of John C. Calhoun,* 10:135–155. Defense of the vice president's policies in presiding over the Senate from attacks by the Adams administration.

**355.** [Calhoun, John C.] *Onslow in Reply to Patrick Henry.* [Washington: printed by the Daily National Intelligencer, 1826]. Pamphlet version of #354.

**356.** "Onslow" to "Patrick Henry," October 7, October 10, and October 12, 1826. *The Papers of John C. Calhoun,* 10:208–221, 223–233. Follow-up to above, not included in pamphlet version.

**357.** "Address to the People of South Carolina," December 1830. *The Papers of John C. Calhoun,* 11:264–280. Draft of a defense of interposition prepared for the South Carolina General Assembly but not used or made public at the time.

**358.** To the People of the United States, February 17, 1831. Washington, D.C., *United States Telegraph,* February 17, 1831; *The Papers of John C. Calhoun,* 11:334–338. The vice president makes public his disagreement with Jackson over the Seminole War controversy and publishes many historical documents in support.

**359.** [Calhoun, John C., ed.] *Correspondence between Gen. Andrew Jackson and John C. Calhoun, President and Vice-President of the U. States, on the Subject of the Course of the Latter, in the Deliberations of the Cabinet of Mr. Monroe, on the Occurrences in the Seminole War.* Washington: printed by Duff Green, 1831. Well-known pamphlet version of #358.

**360.** To the People of the United States, February 24, 1831. Washington, D.C., *United States' Telegraph,* February 25, 1831; *The Papers* *of John C. Calhoun,* 11:342–350. Supplement to the above, not included in the pamphlet version.

**361.** "The Fort Hill Address," July 26, 1831. Pendleton, S.C., *Messenger,* August 3, 1831; *The Papers of John C. Calhoun,* 11:413–440. The vice president makes public his support of interposition and defends it.

**362.** [Calhoun, John C.] *Opinions of the Vice-President of the United States, on the Relation of the States and the General Government.* Charleston, S.C.: printed by E.J. Van Brunt, 1831. Well-known pamphlet version of #361.

**363.** Calhoun, John C. "Reply to John H. Eaton's Address." Pendleton, S.C., *Messenger,* October 19, 1831; *The Papers of John C. Calhoun,* 11:474–482. Calhoun's reluctant public statement on the Peggy Eaton affair.

**364.** Report on Federal Relations, November 1831. *The Papers of John C. Calhoun,* 11:485–509. Further defense of interposition, drafted for the South Carolina General Assembly and not made public at the time.

**365.** To Governor James Hamilton, Jr., August 28, 1832. Pendleton, S.C., *Messenger,* September 15 and 19, 1832; *The Papers of John C. Calhoun,* 11:613–649. Further public exposition of state rights.

**366.** *Important Correspondence on the Subject of State Interposition, between His Excellency Gov. Hamilton, and Hon. John C. Calhoun, Vice-President of the United States.* Charleston, S.C.: printed by A.E. Miller, 1832. Well-known pamphlet version of #365.

**367.** "Address to the People of the United States." November 1832. *The Papers of John C. Calhoun,* 11:669–681. Drafted for the South Carolina General Assembly to accompany the ordinance of nullification, not used at the time.

**368.** Report for a Virginia Commercial Convention, June 14, 1838. *The Papers of John C. Calhoun,* 14:321–343. Discrimination of federal taxation and expenditure against the South and need for direct trade between the South and Europe. A document presented by Francis Mallory, but drafted by Calhoun.

**369.** To William Smith of Virginia, July 3, 1843. *The Papers of John C. Calhoun,* 17:270–291. Essay on the issues of majority rule and constitutionality raised by the "Dorr War" in Rhode Island, not published at the time.

**370.** "The Address of Mr. Calhoun to His Political Friends and Supporters," December 21, 1843. *The Papers of John C. Calhoun,* 17:617–633 and 729–742. Calhoun's original draft of his announcement that he was withdrawing from the Democratic presidential race, and why; and the slightly revised version published by his Charleston campaign committee.

**371.** Calhoun, John C. *Hon. J.C. Calhoun's Letter to the Hon. W.R. King.* Charleston: printed by Walker & Burke [1844]. Calhoun's most extended public statement against British antislavery influence in the New World. A public pamphlet distribution of #344.

**372.** [Calhoun, John C.] *The Address of the Southern Delegates to Their Constituents.* Washington: Towers, 1849; *The Works of John C. Calhoun,* 6:285–313. Position on slavery in the territories, January, 1849.

**373.** Calhoun, John C. *Mr. Calhoun's Address to the People of the Southern States.* [Washington: 1849]. Calhoun's defense of his position on the Mexican War and related issues, July 5, 1849.

## 4. Public Letters (Selected)

**374.** To a Committee at Edgefield, S.C., March 27, 1833; Charleston, S.C., *Mercury,* April 11, 1833. *The Papers of John C. Calhoun,* 12:149–154. On the recent compromise between South Carolina and the federal government.

**375.** To a Committee at Charleston, S.C., March 24, 1835. Charleston, S.C., *Mercury,* March 27, 1835; *The Papers of John C. Calhoun,* 12:525–529. Successes and what remains to be done in reforming the federal government.

**376.** To a Committee at Edgefield, S.C., November 3, 1837. Edgefield, S.C., *Advertiser,* November 16, 1837; *The Papers of John C. Calhoun,* 13:636–641. Explains his renewed association with the Democrats on banking questions.

**377.** To a Committee of Democrats, New York City, June 4, 1840. *The Papers of John C. Calhoun,* 15:266–270. Support for the Democratic party in the pending elections.

**378.** *Letter of the Hon. John C. Calhoun, of South Carolina, U.S. Senator, in Answer to an Invitation from a Committee Appointed by a Convention of the Democratic Republican Electors at the City of New York, to Deliver an Oration on the Celebration of the Sixty-Fourth Anniversary of the Independence of the United States.* New York: Jared W. Bell, [1840]. Pamphlet version of #377.

**379.** To a Committee at West Point, Ga., August 11, 1840. *The Papers of John C. Calhoun,* 15:327–332. The condition and needs of the country.

**380.** To a Committee at Cincinnati, July 9, 1843. Cincinnati *Daily Enquirer,* August 2, 1843; *The Papers of John C. Calhoun,* 17:300–303. The presidency should not be sought by electioneering.

**381.** To a Committee at St. Clairsville, Ohio, September 12, 1844. *The Papers of John C. Calhoun,* 19:757–759. Refuting false charges by the Whigs in regard to his grounds for defense of slavery.

**382.** To a Committee at Mobile, May 15, 1845. Mobile, Ala., *Register and Journal,* May 27, 1845. Review of his service as secretary of state.

**383.** To a Committee in South Carolina, November 1846. *The Works of John C. Calhoun,* 6:254–272. On the South Carolina constitution and the concurrent majority.

# III.
# Biographies of John C. Calhoun

## A. BOOKS

**384.** Capers, Gerald M. *John C. Calhoun, Opportunist: A Reappraisal.* Gainesville, Fla.: University of Florida Press, 1960; Chicago: Quadrangle Books, 1969. Relentlessly hostile and superficial portrayal of Calhoun's career from the viewpoint of contemporary enemies.

**385.** Coit, Margaret L. *John C. Calhoun: American Portrait.* Boston: Houghton Mifflin, 1950 (and later editions). Colorful and sympathetic life and times which won the Pulitzer Prize for Biography. By far the best one-volume treatment.

**386.** Holst, Hermann E., von. *John C. Calhoun.* Boston: Houghton Mifflin, 1882 (and later editions). A highly argumentative portrayal of Calhoun as the evil genius who brought on the Civil War.

**387.** Hunt, Gaillard. *John C. Calhoun.* Philadelphia: George W. Jacobs & Co., 1908. A colorful and interpretive, mildly critical account of Calhoun's career.

**388.** [Hunter, Robert M.T.] *Life of John C. Calhoun. Presenting a Condensed History of Political Events from 1811 to 1843.* New York: Harper & Brothers, 1843. Calhoun's career and American history (up to 1843) told from the viewpoint of a Calhoun admirer; contains otherwise unknown material on early life.

**389.** Jenkins, John S. *The Life of John Caldwell Calhoun.* Auburn, N.Y.: James M. Alden, 1850 (and at least four subsequent editions by other printers). Eulogistic treatment from the point of view of a late antebellum Democratic party publicist.

**390.** Lindsey, David. *Andrew Jackson and John C. Calhoun.* Woodbury, N.Y.: Barrons Educational Series, 1973. Colorful and well-written "dual biography" of two great and rather similar figures of the middle period of American history.

**391.** Meigs, William M. *The Life of John Caldwell Calhoun,* 2 vols. New York: Neale Publishing Co., 1917. A detailed and low-keyed political biography.

**392.** Niven, John. *John C. Calhoun and the Price of Union: A Biography.* Baton Rouge and London: Louisiana State University Press, 1988. Conventional political narrative from the viewpoint of Martin Van Buren Democrats, which adds little to previous fact or theory except the eccentric thesis that Calhoun's politics are explained by an inferiority complex.

**393.** Peterson, Merrill D. *The Great Triumvirate: Webster, Clay, and Calhoun.* New York and Oxford: Oxford University Press, 1987. A vivid but unsympathetic recounting of Calhoun's career as interwoven with those of his great contemporaries.

**394.** Pinckney, Gustavus M. *Life of John C. Calhoun: Being a View of the Principal Events of His Career and an Account of His Contributions to Economic and Political Science.* Charleston, S.C.: Walker, Evans, & Cogswell, 1903. Eulogistic treatment by a Southern admirer.

**395.** Styron, Arthur M. *The Cast-Iron Man: John C. Calhoun and American Democracy.* New York: Longmans, Green and Co., 1935. A sympathetic life and times, tracing Calhoun's relationship to the evolution of democracy through agrarian, popular, national, and industrial stages.

**396.** Wiltse, Charles M. *John C. Calhoun,* 3 vols. Indianapolis: Bobbs Merrill, 1944–1951; New York: Russell & Russell, 1968. Vol. 1: *John C. Calhoun: Nationalist, 1782–1828.* Vol. 2. *John C. Calhoun: Nullifier, 1829–1839.* Vol. 3. *John C. Calhoun: Sectionalist, 1840–1850.* Detailed, well-written, and sympathetic: the standard biography.

## B. SHORT BIOGRAPHICAL TREATMENTS

**397.** Alexander, Holmes. "John Caldwell Calhoun." In Alexander, *The Famous Five.* New York: Bookmailer, 1958. Good popular treatment (pp. 87–121).

**398.** Current, Richard N. "John Caldwell Calhoun." In *Encyclopedia of Southern History.* Edited by David C. Roller and Robert W. Twyman, p. 171. Baton Rouge, La.: Louisiana State University Press, 1979. Concise account of the main points of Calhoun's public life.

**399.** Hammond, James H. "An Oration on the Life, Character, and Services of John Caldwell Calhoun, Delivered on the 21st November, 1850, in Charleston, S.C., at the Request of the City Council." In *Selections from the Letters and Speeches of the Hon. James H. Hammond, of South Carolina,* pp. 231–300. Edited by Clyde N. Wilson. Spartanburg, S.C.: The Reprint Co., 1977. Calhoun's life and American history ably reviewed from the standpoint of antebellum South Carolina.

**400.** Harrison, Lowell H. "'A Cast-Iron Man': John C. Calhoun." *American History Illustrated* 9 (February 1975): 4–9, 43–49. Accurate and well-illustrated biographical treatment from a human-interest standpoint.

**401.** Kendrick, Benjamin B. "John Caldwell Calhoun." *Encyclopedia Britannica,* 14th edition. 24 vols. New York: Encyclopedia Britannica Inc., 1929–1930, 4:584–585. Brief biography and full and balanced, though concise, review of the motives and ideas that characterized Calhoun's career.

**402.** Parton, James. "John C. Calhoun." In Parton, *Famous Americans of Recent Times,* pp. 113–171. Boston: Ticknor & Fields, 1867 (and later editions). Writing very much in the shadow of the Civil War, America's first professional biographer portrayed Calhoun's career in terms of "loathsome and despicable" motives.

**403.** Phillips, Ulrich B. "John Caldwell Calhoun." In *Dictionary of American Biography,* 22 vols. New York: Charles Scribner's Sons, 1928–1944, 3:411–419. A short account of Calhoun's career, packed with facts and astute judgments. With #407 the best short treatment.

**404.** Seitz, Don C. *The "Also Rans": Great Men Who Missed Making the Presidential Goal.* Freeport, N.Y.: Books for Librarians, 1968 (reprint of 1928 edition). Very shallow and popularized treatment of Calhoun (pp. 53–76).

**405.** Southwick, Leslie H. *Presidential Also Rans and Running Mates, 1788–1980.* Jefferson, N.C., and London: McFarland Co., 1984. Quite good and thoughtful though brief life of Calhoun (pp. 80–87).

**406.** Thomas, Emory M. "John C. Calhoun." In *Encyclopedia of Southern Culture*. Edited by Charles Reagan Wilson and William Ferris, pp. 1183–1184. Chapel Hill, N.C. and London: University of North Carolina Press, 1989. A succinct summary of Calhoun's life and lasting importance.

**407.** Wilson, Clyde N. "John Caldwell Calhoun." In *Antebellum Writers in New York and the South*. Edited by Joel Myerson. (Vol. 3 of *Dictionary of Literary Biography*), pp. 44–55. Detroit: Gale Research Co., 1979. Calhoun's life framed by his major speeches and writings. With #403 the best short treatment.

# IV.
# Background and Early Life (to 1811)

### A. THE CALHOUNS AND RELATED FAMILIES

**408.** "The Caldwells of Mill Creek, Newberry." Newberry, S.C., *Observer,* April 28, 1887. Information on Calhoun's mother's family.

**409.** Calhoun, Orval A. *800 Years of Colquhoun, Colhoun, Calhoun, and Cahoon Family History in Ireland, Scotland, England, United States of America, Australia, and Canada.* 3 vols. Baltimore: Gateway Press, 1976–1987.

**410.** Clower, George Wesley. "Notes on the Calhoun-Noble-Davis Family." *South Carolina Historical Magazine* 53 (January 1952): 51–52. Supplement to Salley (#418).

**411.** Draper, Lyman C., comp. "Calhoun Settlement." *Gulf States Historical Magazine* 1 (July 1902): 439–441. Calhoun's own account of his family history, given in 1847 and collected many years later from an Abbeville, S.C., newspaper editor to whom he had related it.

**412.** Dundas, F. de Sales. *The Calhoun Settlement. District of Abbeville, South Carolina.* Staunton, Va.: privately printed, 1949. Useful material on Calhoun's ancestry, relatives, and native region.

**413.** "Inscriptions from a Calhoun Burying Ground." *South Carolina Historical Magazine* 27 (July 1926): 184–187. Records of Calhoun's parents and other close relatives.

**414.** Kemper, Charles E. "The Calhoun Ancestry." *William and Mary Quarterly,* 2nd series 6 (January 1926): 53–54 and 7 (January 1927): 57–59.

**415.** *Life and Character of the Hon. John C. Calhoun, with Illustrations: Containing Notices of His Father and Uncles, and Their Brave Conduct During Our Struggle for Independence, in the American Revolutionary War.* New York: J. Winchester, New World Press, [1843]. Short popular life, illustrated by woodcuts, with the emphasis on Calhoun's immediate ancestry.

**416.** McPherson, Lewin Dwinell. *Calhoun, Hamilton, Baskin, and Related Families.* Privately produced, 1957. Extended genealogical study.

**417.** O'Neall, John Belton. *The Annals of Newberry.* Charleston, S.C.: S.G. Courtenay & Co., 1859. Information on Calhoun-related families.

**418.** Salley, Alexander S. "The Calhoun Family of South Carolina." *South Carolina Historical Magazine* 7 (April 1906): 81–98 and (July 1906): 153–169. Detailed account of Calhoun's ancestry, collateral relatives, and descendants.

**419.** ———. "The Grandfather of John C. Calhoun." *South Carolina Historical Magazine* 39 (January 1938): 50. Patrick Calhoun, the immigrant from Ireland.

**420.** Watson, Margaret. *Greenwood County Sketches: Old Roads and Early Families.* Greenwood, S.C.: Attic Press, Inc., n.d. Account of many Calhoun collateral ancestors and relatives (pp. 174–181).

## B. UPCOUNTRY SOUTH CAROLINA

**421.** Bacot, D. Huger. "The South Carolina Upcountry at the End of the Eighteenth Century." *American Historical Review* 28 (July 1923): 682–698. The time and region of Calhoun's birth and childhood.

**422.** Howe, George. *History of the Presbyterian Church in South Carolina.* 2 vols. Charleston, S.C.: Walker, Evans and Cogswell, 1883. The Scotch-Irish in the South Carolina upcountry.

**423.** Logan, John H. *History of the Upper Country of South Carolina, from the Earliest Period to the Close of the War of Independence.* Charleston, S.C.: S.G. Courtenay & Co., 1859 (and several reprint editions).

**Background and Early Life (to 1811)**

424. Meriwether, Robert L. *Expansion of South Carolina, 1729-1765.* Kingsport, Tenn.: Southern Publishers, 1940. Settlement of the South Carolina upcountry by Calhouns and others before Calhoun's birth.

425. Robertson, Ben. *Red Hills and Cotton: An Upcountry Memory.* New York: 1942; Columbia: University of South Carolina Press, 1960 (and later editions). Classic evocation of the spirit of Calhoun's native region.

## C. EARLY LIFE AND EDUCATION

426. Coit, Margaret L. "Moses Waddel: A Light in the Wilderness." *Georgia Review* 5 (Spring 1951): 34-47. The teacher of Calhoun and other famous Southerners.

427. Davis, Mary Katherine. "The Featherbed Aristocracy: Abbeville District in the 1790's." *South Carolina Historical Magazine* 80 (April 1979): 136-155. The civilizational progress of Calhoun's locale during his childhood.

428. Starke, William Pinkney. "Account of Calhoun's Early Life, Abridged from the Manuscript of Col. W. Pinkney Starke." In J. Franklin Jameson, ed., *Correspondence of John C. Calhoun (American Historical Association Annual Report* for 1899), vol. 2, pp. 65-89. Washington: U.S. Government Printing Office, 1900. Uninspired, but written with access to family lore and papers.

429. Waddel, John Newton. *Memorials of Academic Life: Being an Historical Sketch of the Waddel Family.* Richmond: Presbyterian Publications Committee, 1891. On Moses Waddel, Calhoun's teacher and brother-in-law.

430. Wade, John Donald. *Augustus Baldwin Longstreet: A Study of the Development of Culture in the South.* New York: Macmillan, 1924; Athens, Ga.: University of Georgia Press, 1969. This biography of the author A.B. Longstreet, like Calhoun a student of Moses Waddel, gives perhaps the best description of Waddel's famous academy.

## D. YALE COLLEGE

**431.** Barber, John Warner. *Views of New Haven and Its Vicinity.* New Haven: Barber & Maltby, 1825. Well-illustrated description of Yale and New Haven in Calhoun's time.

**432.** Dexter, Franklin B. "Student Life at Yale College under the First President Dwight." *American Antiquarian Society Proceedings,* new series 27 (1917): 318–335.

**433.** Fisher, George P. *Life of Benjamin Silliman,* 2 vols. New York: Charles Scribner & Co., 1866. Calhoun's relationship with the famous scientist and Yale professor.

**434.** Kevlin, Thomas Anthony. "The Religious and Political Thought of Timothy Dwight." M.A. thesis, University of South Carolina, 1970. Calhoun's teacher.

**435.** "Mr. Calhoun and His College Contemporaries." Charleston, S.C., *Courier,* April 23, 1840. This unsigned article contains a number of interesting details about Calhoun's college days and classmates.

**436.** Stokes, Anson Phelps. *Memoirs of Eminent Yale Men,* 2 vols. New Haven, Conn.: Yale University Press, 1914. Calhoun (2:196–206).

## E. LEGAL EDUCATION AND LAW PRACTICE

**437.** Easterby, J. Harold. "Henry William De Saussure." In *Dictionary of American Biography,* Edited by Allen Johnson and Dumas Malone. 22 vols. New York: Charles Scribner's Sons, 1928–1944, 5:253–254. Calhoun's Charleston law mentor.

**438.** Fisher, Samuel Herbert. *The Litchfield Law School, 1775-1833.* New Haven, Conn.: Yale University Press, 1933. Description of the institution.

**439.** Kilbourn, Dwight C. *The Bench and Bar of Litchfield County, Connecticut, 1709–1909.* Litchfield, Conn.: privately printed, 1909. Catalog of Calhoun's classmates at the Litchfield Law School, pp. 195–214.

**440.** Meleney, John C. "The Public Life of Aedanus Burke: Revolutionary Republican in Post-Revolutionary South Carolina." Ph.D. dis-

# Background and Early Life (to 1811)

sertation, University of South Carolina, 1988. Law and politics in Calhoun's formative period in this study of a leading jurist.

**441.** O'Neall, John Belton. *Biographical Sketches of the Bench and Bar of South Carolina.* 2 vols. Charleston, S.C.: S.G. Courtenay & Co., 1859. In-depth and first-hand view of the personnel of the legal profession.

**442.** Perry, Benjamin F. "Henry William De Saussure." In *The Writings of Benjamin F. Perry.* Edited by Stephen Meats and Edwin T. Arnold, 3 vols. Spartanburg, S.C.: Reprint Co., 1980, 2:173–176. Calhoun's Charleston law mentor.

**443.** Rogers, George C., Jr. *Charleston in the Age of the Pinckneys.* Norman, Okla.: University of Oklahoma Press, 1969; reprint, Columbia, S.C.: University of South Carolina Press, 1980. The city of Calhoun's youthful law studies and courtship.

**444.** Watkins, F.T. "John C. Calhoun: Attorney at Law." *South Carolina Bar Association Transactions* 41 (1934): 110–116. Aspects of Calhoun's brief early law practice.

## F. SOUTH CAROLINA POLITICS IN THE EARLY NINETEENTH CENTURY

**445.** Kaplanoff, Mark D. "Making the South Solid: Politics and the Structure of Society in South Carolina, 1790–1815." Ph.D. dissertation, Cambridge University, 1979. Original and penetrating view of forces, personalities, and ideas.

**446.** Rangila, Nancy A. "South Carolina: The Growth of Nationalism, 1805–1815." M.A. thesis, University of South Carolina, 1964.

**447.** Rogers, George C., Jr. *Evolution of a Federalist: William Loughton Smith of Charleston (1758–1812).* Columbia, S.C.: University of South Carolina Press, 1962. South Carolina politics in the immediate pre-Calhoun period.

**448.** Shand, William Munro, III. "The Image of Thomas Jefferson as Seen by South Carolinians, 1800–1826." M.A. thesis, University of South Carolina, 1977.

**449.** Starr, Raymond G. "The Conservative Revolution: South Carolina Public Affairs, 1775–1790." Ph.D. dissertation, University of Texas, 1964.

**450.** Williams, Frances Leigh. *A Founding Family: The Pinckneys of South Carolina.* New York: Harcourt Brace Jovanovich, 1978.

**451.** Wolfe, John Harold. *Jeffersonian Democracy in South Carolina.* Chapel Hill, N.C.: University of North Carolina Press, 1940.

## G. CALHOUN'S PUBLIC LIFE TO 1811

**452.** Bowie, Alexander. "Brief Sketch of Mr. Calhoun." Camden, S.C., *Journal*, October 24, 1854. Recollections of a companion during Calhoun's early political life.

**453.** [Maxcy, Virgil.] "Biographical Memoir of John Caldwell Calhoun." Washington *United States' Telegraph,* April 25 and 26, 1831. A sketch of Calhoun's ancestry, education, and early public career by an intimate youthful friend—source of much later writing on Calhoun's early life.

**454.** Meriwether, Robert L. Introduction to Meriwether, ed., *The Papers of John C. Calhoun,* vol. 1, *1801–1817,* pp. xxiii–xxxiii. Columbia: University of South Carolina Press, 1959. Succinct overview of Calhoun's background and early political career.

# V.
# Public Career of John C. Calhoun

## A. HISTORICAL BACKGROUND

### 1. National Politics

**455.** Clark, Victor S. "The Influence of Manufactures upon Political Sentiment in the United States from 1820 to 1860." *American Historical Review* 22 (October 1916): 58–64.

**456.** Craven, Avery O. *The Coming of the Civil War.* Chicago: University of Chicago Press, 1942. Critical view of Calhoun as a catalyst of needless sectional conflict.

**457.** Cunliffe, Marcus. *The Nation Takes Shape, 1789–1837.* Chicago: University of Chicago Press, 1959. Period survey.

**458.** Fehrenbacher, Don E. *The Era of Expansion, 1800–1848.* New York: John Wiley & Sons, Inc., 1969. Excellent survey of the basic characteristics, events, and issues of the "Jeffersonian" and "Jacksonian" eras.

**459.** Heale, M.J. *The Presidential Quest: Candidates and Images in American Political Culture, 1787–1852.* London and New York: Longman, 1982. Conventional and very superficial treatment of Calhoun as a presidential contender.

**460.** Lloyd, Arthur Young. *The Slavery Controversy, 1831–1860.* Chapel Hill, N.C.: University of North Carolina Press, 1939. Old standard.

**461.** McCormick, Richard P. *The Second American Party System: Party Formation in the Jacksonian Era.* Chapel Hill, N.C.: University of North Carolina Press, 1966. Emphasizes the state-specific nature of national parties and the non-involvement of South Carolina with the party system.

**462.** Miles, Edwin A. "The Jacksonian Era." In *Writing Southern History: Essays in Historiography in Honor of Fletcher M. Green,* pp. 125–146. Edited by Arthur S. Link and Rembert W. Patrick. Baton Rouge, La.: Louisiana State University Press, 1965. Excellent historiographical survey up to the date of publication.

**463.** Schlesinger, Arthur M., Jr. *History of American Presidential Elections, 1789–1968.* 4 vols. New York: Chelsea House, 1971.

**464.** Turner, Frederick Jackson. *The Significance of Sections in American History.* New York: Henry Holt, 1920. Classic statement of the fundamentally sectional nature of American history in the 19th century.

**465.** ———. *The United States, 1830–1850: The Nation and Its Sections.* New York: Henry Holt, 1935. Basic account of American history in the Jackson era.

**466.** Welter, Rush. *The Mind of America, 1820–1860.* New York and London: Columbia University Press, 1975. On the centrality of state rights.

**467.** Wiltse, Charles M. *The New Nation, 1800–1845.* New York: Hill & Wang, 1961. Good period survey.

## 2. The South

**468.** Brown, William Garrott. *The Lower South in American History.* New York: Macmillan Co., 1903. Classic interpretation of the unique features of the Deep South.

**469.** Cooper, William J., Jr. *Liberty and Slavery: Southern Politics to 1860.* New York: Alfred A. Knopf, 1983. Convincing argument for the continuity of Southern political interests and beliefs from early colonial times to Calhoun and after.

**470.** ———. *The South and the Politics of Slavery, 1828–1856.* Baton Rouge, La.: Louisiana State University Press, 1978.

**471.** Doherty, Herbert J., Jr. "The Mind of the Antebellum South." In *Writing Southern History: Essays in Historiography in Honor of Fletcher M. Green*. pp. 198–223. Baton Rouge, La.: Louisiana State University Press, 1965. Excellent survey of historical literature up to 1964.

**472.** Eaton, Clement. *The Growth of Southern Civilization, 1790–1860*. New York: Harper & Row, 1961. Calhoun's thought in context: the harmonizing of slavery and democracy.

**473.** Gray, Lewis Cecil. *History of Agriculture in the Southern United States to 1860*. 2 vols. Washington: Carnegie Institution, 1933; several reprint editions. Classic description and analysis of the fundamental basis of antebellum Southern life.

**474.** Green, Fletcher M. *Constitutional Development in the South Atlantic States, 1776–1860*. Chapel Hill, N.C.: University of North Carolina Press, 1930. Classic study of the progressive democratization of Southern state constitutions.

**475.** Luraghi, Raimondo. *The Rise and Fall of the Plantation South*. New York: Franklin Watts, 1978. The Old South neither feudal nor capitalist, but a "seignurial" society marked by aristocratic ethics.

**476.** McCardell, John. *The Idea of a Southern Nation: Southern Nationalists and Southern Nationalism, 1830–1860*. New York: W.W. Norton & Co., 1979.

**477.** Phillips, Ulrich Bonnell. *The Course of the South to Secession*. New York: D. Appleton-Century, 1939.

**478.** Russell, Robert R. *Economic Aspects of Southern Sectionalism, 1840–1861*. Urbana, Ill.: University of Illinois Press, 1924.

**479.** Simkins, Francis Butler, and Charles P. Roland. *A History of the South*. New York: Alfred A. Knopf, 1972. Many brilliantly formulated insights into Southern history.

**480.** Sydnor, Charles S. *The Development of Southern Sectionalism, 1819–1848* (Vol. 5 of *A History of the South*). Baton Rouge, La.: Louisiana State University Press, 1948. Exhaustive history of the South during Calhoun's era.

**481.** Wood, Walter Kirk. "The Central Theme of Southern History: Republicanism, Not Slavery, Race, or Romanticism." *Continuity: A Journal of History* 9 (Fall 1984): 33–71. An interpretation of the "central theme" of Southern history built around Calhoun.

### 3. South Carolina

*a. General*

**482.** Chesnutt, David R., and Clyde N. Wilson, eds. *The Meaning of South Carolina History: Essays in Honor of George C. Rogers, Jr.* Columbia, S.C.: University of South Carolina Press, 1990. Twelve historians explore the unique features of South Carolina history from colonial times to the recent past.

**483.** Guess, William Francis. *South Carolina: Annals of Pride and Protest.* New York: Harper, 1960. Impressionistic popular history.

**484.** Mills, Robert. *Atlas of the State of South Carolina.* Baltimore: F. Lucas, Jr., 1825. Information on geography and transportation in Calhoun's time.

**485.** Rogers, George C., Jr. "South Carolina." In *The Encyclopedia of Southern History.* Edited by David C. Roller and Robert W. Twyman, pp. 1126–1143. Baton Rouge, La.: Louisiana State University Press, 1979. South Carolina history as a unique experiment in race relations of long duration and a search for balance and continuity.

**486.** Rogers, George C., Jr. *A South Carolina Chronology, 1497–1970.* Columbia, S.C.: University of South Carolina Press, 1973.

**487.** Wallace, David Duncan. *South Carolina: A Short History, 1520–1948.* Chapel Hill: University of North Carolina Press, 1951. Detailed standard history.

*b. Politics*

**488.** Bailey, N. Louise, Mary L. Morgan, and Carolyn R. Taylor, *Biographical Directory of the South Carolina Senate, 1776–1985.* 3 vols. Columbia: University of South Carolina Press, 1986.

**489.** Boucher, Chauncey S. "Sectionalism, Representation, and the Electoral Question in Antebellum South Carolina." *Washington University Studies* 4 (October 1916): 3–62.

**490.** Coussons, John S. "Thirty Years with Calhoun, Rhett, and the Charleston *Mercury:* A Chapter in South Carolina Politics." Ph.D. dissertation, Louisiana State University, 1971. A study of the newspaper that usually spoke for Calhoun.

**491.** Edgar, Walter B., Louis N. Bailey, et al., eds. *Biographical Directory of the South Carolina House of Representatives.* 4 vols. to date. Columbia, S.C.: University of South Carolina Press, 1974–.

**492.** Ford, Lacy K. *Origins of Southern Radicalism: The South Carolina Upcountry, 1800–1860.* New York and Oxford: Oxford University Press, 1988. In-depth socioeconomic and ideological study of Calhoun's home region as the seedbed of Southern political militancy.

**493.** Greenberg, Kenneth S. "The Second American Revolution: South Carolina Politics, Society, and Secession, 1776–1860." Ph.D. dissertation, University of Wisconsin, 1976. The continuity of South Carolina politics as a unit against the world.

**494.** Moltke-Hansen, David. "Protecting Interests, Maintaining Rights, Emulating Ancestors: U.S. Constitution Bicentennial Reflections on 'The Problem of South Carolina,' 1787–1860." *South Carolina Historical Magazine* 89 (July 1988): 160–182. Facets of the unique continuity of South Carolina political behavior explored.

**495.** Perry, Benjamin F. *The Writings of Benjamin F. Perry.* Edited by Stephen Meats and Edwin T. Arnold. 3 vols. Spartanburg, S.C.: Reprint Co., 1980. Includes, besides other material, the 1882 and 1889 *Reminiscences of Public Men* with many first-hand character sketches of Calhoun's contemporaries by a prominent South Carolina editor and politician.

**496.** Prior, Granville T. "A History of the Charleston Mercury, 1822–1852." Ph.D. dissertation, Harvard University, 1947. History of the most important press associate of Calhoun's political career.

**497.** Reynolds, Emily B., and Joan Reynolds Faunt. *Biographical Directory of the Senate of South Carolina, 1776–1964.* Columbia, S.C.: South Carolina Department of Archives and History, 1964.

**498.** Schaper, William A. "Sectionalism and Representation in South Carolina." In *Annual Report of the American Historical Association* for 1900, 2:237–463. Washington: U.S. Government Printing Office, 1901. Classic study of the distribution of political power within South Carolina.

**499.** Weir, Robert M. "'The Harmony We Were Famous For': An Interpretation of Pre-Revolutionary South Carolina Politics." *William and Mary Quarterly* 26 (October 1969): 473–501. The origins of the unusual unity of political action in South Carolina, with important implications for Calhoun's time.

**500.** Weir, Robert M. "The South Carolinian as Extremist." *South Atlantic Quarterly* 74 (December 1975): 86–103. Sophisticated analysis of a continuing phenomenon.

*c. Economics*

**501.** Boucher, Chauncey S. "The Antebellum Attitude of South Carolina Towards Manufacturing and Agriculture." *Washington University Studies* 3 (April 1916): 243–270.

**502.** Clark, W.A. *The History of Banking Institutions Organized in South Carolina Prior to 1860.* Columbia, S.C.: The State Co., 1922. Always a lively public issue in the state in Calhoun's time.

**503.** Coclanis, Peter A. *The Shadow of a Dream: Economic Life and Death in the South Carolina Low Country, 1670–1920.* New York and Oxford: Oxford University Press, 1989. The long and unique economic history of the South Carolina low country.

**504.** Mills, Robert. *Statistics of South Carolina.* Charleston, S.C.: Hurlbut and Lloyd, 1826. Economic picture.

**505.** Smith, Alfred Glaze. *Economic Readjustment of an Old Cotton State: South Carolina, 1820–1860.* Columbia, S.C.: University of South Carolina Press, 1958.

**506.** Van Deusen, John G. *Economic Bases of Disunion in South Carolina.* New York: Columbia University Press, 1928. Nullification related to agricultural decline.

*d. Society and Culture*

**507.** Burton, Orville Vernon. *In My Father's House are Many Mansions: Family and Community in Edgefield, South Carolina.* Chapel Hill, N.C. and London: University of North Carolina Press, 1985. Intensive study of a region famous for its fire-eaters, which was a part of Calhoun's early congressional district and the residence of many Calhoun relatives and supporters.

**508.** Davidson, Chalmers Gaston. *The Last Foray: The South Carolina Planters of 1860, A Sociological Study.* Columbia, S.C.: University of South Carolina Press, 1971. Includes many Calhoun relatives and supporters and an interesting social portrait of the predominant class.

**509.** Joyner, Charles W. *Down by the Riverside: A South Carolina Slave Community.* Urbana, Ill.: University of Illinois Press, 1984. Brilliant study of black life in South Carolina's unique rice region.

**510.** O'Brien, Michael, and David Moltke-Hansen, eds. *Intellectual Life in Antebellum Charleston.* Knoxville, Tenn.: University of Tennessee Press, 1986. A dozen historians examine aspects of culture and ideology in South Carolina from the Constitution to secession.

**511.** Rogers, George C., Jr. *The History of Georgetown County, South Carolina.* Columbia, S.C.: University of South Carolina Press, 1970. In-depth study of South Carolina's unique rice plantation region.

**512.** Taylor, Rosser H. *Antebellum South Carolina: A Social and Cultural History.* Chapel Hill, N.C.: University of North Carolina Press, 1942.

**4. Relevant Studies of Other States**

**513.** Ambler, Charles H. *Thomas Ritchie: A Study in Virginia Politics.* Richmond: Bell Books, 1913. The gray eminence of Virginia politics in Calhoun's time.

**514.** Darling, Arthur B. *Political Changes in Massachusetts, 1824–1848. A Study of Liberal Movements in Politics.* New Haven, Conn.: Yale University Press, 1925. Useful material on Calhoun's relationship to the various Democratic factions of Massachusetts.

**515.** Miles, Edwin A. *Jacksonian Democracy in Mississippi*. Chapel Hill, N.C.: University of North Carolina Press, 1960.

**516.** Phillips, Ulrich B. *Georgia and State Rights: A Study of the Political History of Georgia from the Revolution to the Civil War*. In *American Historical Association Annual Report* for 1901, pp. 3–220. Washington: U.S. Government Printing Office, 1902.

**517.** Thornton, J. Mills. *Politics and Power in a Slave Society: Alabama, 1800–1860*. Baton Rouge, La. and London: Louisiana State University Press, 1978. The political ideas, factions, and evolution of a state influenced by Calhoun.

**518.** Wagstaff, Henry M. *State Rights and Political Parties in North Carolina, 1776–1861*. Baltimore: Johns Hopkins Press, 1906.

## B. U.S. HOUSE OF REPRESENTATIVES, 1811–1817

### 1. General

**519.** Adams, Henry. *History of the United States of America During the Administrations of Thomas Jefferson and James Madison*. 9 vols. New York: Scribners, 1889–1891. Volumes 6–9 of this classic treatment of the Jeffersonian era pay balanced attention to Calhoun's role as a legislative leader.

**520.** Brant, Irving. *James Madison*. 6 vols. Indianapolis: Bobbs-Merrill, 1940–1961. The last two volumes of this standard biography, dealing with Madison's presidency, rather slight Calhoun's role in the period.

**521.** Kennedy, John F. *Profiles in Courage*. New York: Harper & Row, 1955 (and many later editions). Many scattered comments on Calhoun, the most interesting in regard to his courage in defending a congressional pay raise to his constituents in 1816 (pp. 251–252).

**522.** Ravenel, Mrs. St. Julien. *Life and Times of William Lowndes of South Carolina, 1782–1822*. Boston: Houghton, Mifflin & Co., 1901. Biography of a South Carolinian who was Calhoun's close friend and political ally in the early part of his career.

**523.** Risjord, Norman K. *The Old Republicans: Southern Conservatives in the Age of Jefferson*. New York: Columbia University Press, 1965. "Old Republican" opposition to Calhoun's "nationalism."

**524.** Vipperman, Carl J. *William Lowndes and the Transition of Southern Politics, 1782–1822.* Chapel Hill, N.C. and London: University of North Carolina Press, 1989. Important study of Calhoun's "War Hawk" colleague from South Carolina and of the evolution of Southern republicanism in the era of the War of 1812.

## 2. The War of 1812

**525.** Hunt, Gaillard. "Joseph Gales on the War Manifesto of 1812." *American Historical Review* 13 (January 1908): 303–310. Argues against Calhoun's authorship of the declaration of war. (See #532)

**526.** Ingersoll, Charles J. *Historical Sketch of the Second War between the United States of America and Great Britain.* 3 vols. Philadelphia: Lea & Blanchard, 1845–1852. History of the era by an eyewitness and associate of Calhoun in the House.

**527.** Latimer, Margaret K. "South Carolina—A Protagonist of the War of 1812." *American Historical Review* 61 (1956): 914–929. The key role of Calhoun and other South Carolina political leaders in bringing on and conducting the war.

**528.** Pratt, Julius W. *Expansionists of 1812.* New York: Macmillan, 1925. Classic study of the "War Hawks."

**529.** Stephenson, Nathaniel W. "Calhoun, 1812, and After." *American Historical Review* 31 (July 1926): 701–707. Profound analysis of the "War Hawk" legacy and the failure of its nationalist aspirations.

**530.** Tozawa, Kenji. ["John C. Calhoun and the War of 1812."] *Ehime Law Journal* 12 (July 1985): 49–91. Japanese perspective, part of a prospective biography.

**531.** Wiltse, Charles M. "The Authorship of the War Report of 1812." *American Historical Review* 49 (January 1944): 253–259. Circumstances surrounding Calhoun's drafting of the key document justifying the declaration of war.

## 3. Postwar Issues

**532.** Adams, Porter H. "The Tariff of 1816 with Special Emphasis on the Views of John C. Calhoun." M.A. thesis, University of South

Carolina, 1966. Analysis of a key legislative issue with later implications.

**533.** Catterall, Ralph H. *Second Bank of the United States.* Chicago: University of Chicago Press, 1903. Calhoun's role in the chartering and design of the national bank in 1816.

**534.** *A Letter to Mr. Calhoun, Chairman of the Committee on a National Currency.* Philadelphia: M. Carey, 1816. Protest of some banking interests against the hard money provisions of Calhoun's national bank plan.

**535.** Preyer, Norris W. "Southern Support for the Tariff of 1816—A Reappraisal." *Journal of Southern History* 25 (May 1959): 306–322. Reexamination of a key issue.

**536.** Walters, Raymond, Jr. *Alexander James Dallas.* Philadelphia: University of Pennsylvania Press, 1943. Biography of the secretary of the treasury at the time of the planning of the national bank.

## C. SECRETARY OF WAR, 1817–1825

### 1. The Monroe Cabinet and Administration

**537.** Ammon, Harry. *James Monroe: the Quest for National Identity.* New York: McGraw-Hill, 1971. The context of Calhoun's service in the Monroe cabinet.

**538.** ———. "The Monroe Doctrine: Domestic Politics or National Decision?" *Diplomatic History* 5 (Winter 1981): 53–70. The formulation of the famous policy by the Monroe cabinet.

**539.** Dangerfield, George. *The Era of Good Feelings.* New York: Harcourt, Brace & Co., 1952. Colorful general account of the Monroe period and the election of 1824.

**540.** Moore, Glover. *The Missouri Controversy, 1819–1821.* Lexington, Ky.: University Press of Kentucky, 1966. Classic account of one of the major events of the Monroe years.

**541.** Perkins, Dexter. *The Monroe Doctrine, 1823–1826.* Cambridge, Mass.: Harvard University Press, 1927 (and later editions). Standard study of one of the major issues.

**542.** Turner, Frederick Jackson. *The Rise of the New West, 1819–1829.* New York and London: Harper, 1906. Standard account of the Monroe years.

**543.** White, Leonard D. *The Jeffersonians: A Study in Administrative History, 1801–1829.* New York: Macmillan, 1951. Calhoun's career in the War Department in context of his party and period.

## 2. The War Department

**544.** Bell, William Gardner. *Secretaries of War and Secretaries of the Army. Portraits and Biographical Sketches.* Washington: Center for Military History, 1982. Brief treatment of Calhoun, pp. 38–39, 172.

**545.** Hemphill, W. Edwin. Preface and Introduction to Hemphill, ed., *The Papers of John C. Calhoun,* vol. 2, *1817–1818,* pp. ii–xciv. Columbia, S.C.: University of South Carolina Press, 1963. Overview of Calhoun's career as secretary of war.

**546.** ———. Introduction to Hemphill, ed., *The Papers of John C. Calhoun,* vol. 3, *1818–1819,* pp. xiii–xxxiii. Columbia, S.C.: University of South Carolina Press, 1967. Elucidates aspects of Calhoun's service as head of the War Department.

**547.** ———. Introduction to Hemphill, ed., *The Papers of John C. Calhoun,* vol. 4, *1819–1820,* pp. xv–xx. Columbia, S.C.: University of South Carolina Press, 1969.

**548.** ———. Introduction to Hemphill, ed., *The Papers of John C. Calhoun,* vol. 5, *1820–1821,* pp. xi–xxx. Columbia, S.C.: University of South Carolina Press, 1971. Elucidates aspects of Calhoun's administration of the War Department.

**549.** ———. Introduction to Hemphill, ed., *The Papers of John C. Calhoun,* vol. 6, *1821–1822,* pp. ix–xvii. Columbia, S.C.: University of South Carolina Press, 1972. Elucidates aspects of Calhoun's supervision of the War Department.

**550.** Ingersoll, L.D. *A History of the War Department of the United States, with Biographical Sketches of the Secretaries.* Washington: Francis B. Mohun, 1879. Brief overview (pp. 460–467).

**551.** "Sketch of the Life of J.C. Calhoun, Vice-President of the United States." *The Casket* 3 (March 1827): 81–82. Complimentary first-hand account of Calhoun's early public career, especially his accomplishments in the War Department.

**552.** Smith, Carlton B. "John C. Calhoun, Secretary of War, 1817–1825: The Cast-Iron Man as an Administrator." In John B. Boles, ed., *America, the Middle Period: Essays in Honor of Bernard Mayo*, pp. 132–144. Charlottesville, Va.: University Press of Virginia, 1973. Overview of Calhoun's accomplishments as administrator.

**553.** Spiller, Roger J. et al., eds. *Dictionary of American Military Biography.* Westport, Conn.: Greenwood Press, 1984. Secretary of War Calhoun, 3:147–151.

**554.** Young, Frances Packard. "John C. Calhoun as Secretary of War, 1817–1825." *Oregon Historical Society Quarterly* 13 (September 1912): 297–337. A brief overview from secondary sources.

## 3. Military Policy and Administration

**555.** Ambrose, Stephen E. *Duty, Honor, Country: A History of West Point.* Baltimore: Johns Hopkins Press, 1966. The Military Academy during Calhoun's administration of the War Department (pp. 38–105).

**556.** Barsness, Richard W. "John C. Calhoun and the Military Establishment, 1817–1825." *Wisconsin Magazine of History* 50 (Autumn 1966): 43–53.

**557.** Heitman, Francis B. *Historical Register and Dictionary of the United States Army, from Its Organization, September 29, 1789, to March 2, 1903.* 2 vols. Washington: U.S. Government Printing Office, 1903. Personnel and organization of the Army under Calhoun.

**558.** James, Marquis. *Andrew Jackson: The Border Captain.* Indianapolis: Bobbs-Merrill, 1933. Vivid popular treatment of Jackson when he was Calhoun's subordinate.

**559.** Prucha, Francis Paul. *A Guide to the Military Posts of the United States, 1789–1895.* Madison, Wis.: State Historical Society of Wisconsin, 1964. Installations of the Army under Calhoun.

**560.** ———. *The Sword of the Republic: the United States Army on the Frontier, 1783–1846.* New York: Macmillan, 1969.

**561.** Richards, George H. *Memoir of Alexander Macomb, the Major General Commanding the Army of the United States.* New York: McElrath & Bangs, 1832. A major figure in the Army.

**562.** Scott, Winfield. *Memoirs of Lieut.-General Scott.* 2 vols. New York: Sheldon & Co., 1864; reprint, Freeport, N.Y.: Books for Libraries, 1970. Another major (and troublesome) figure in the Army.

**563.** Spiller, Roger J. "Calhoun's Expansible Army: The History of a Military Idea." *South Atlantic Quarterly* 79 (Spring 1980): 189–203. One of the most important aspects of Calhoun's administration.

**564.** ———. "John C. Calhoun as Secretary of War, 1817–1825." Ph.D. dissertation, Louisiana State University, 1977. Calhoun's relationship to the Army in detail.

**565.** Upton, Emory. *The Military Policy of the United States.* Washington: U.S. Government Printing Office, 1917.

**566.** Weigley, Russell F. "John C. Calhoun: The Expansible Army Plan." In Weigley, *Towards an American Army: Military Thought from Washington to Marshall,* pp. 30–37. New York and London: Columbia University Press, 1962.

**567.** Wesley, Edgar B. *Guarding the Frontier; A Study of Frontier Defense from 1815 to 1825.* Minneapolis: University of Minnesota Press, 1935; reprint, Westport, Conn.: Greenwood Press, 1970.

### 4. Indian Policy and Administration

**568.** Abel, Annie H. "History of Indian Consolidation West of the Mississippi." In *American Historical Association Annual Report* for 1906, vol. 1, pp. 233–250. Washington: U.S. Government Printing Office, 1908.

**569.** Catlin, George. *Indians of the Western Frontier: Paintings of George Catlin.* Edited by George I. Quimby. Chicago: Chicago Museum of Natural History, 1954. The remarkable series of Indian portraits initiated by Secretary of War Calhoun.

**570.** De Rosier, Arthur H. "John C. Calhoun and the Removal of the Choctaw Indians." *Proceedings of the South Carolina Historical Association for 1957*: 33–45. Aspects of Indian policy.

**571.** ———. *The Removal of the Choctaw Indians.* Knoxville, Tenn.: University of Tennessee Press, 1970.

**572.** Hemphill, Susan L. "Mission Schools for the Choctaws, 1818–1834." M.A. thesis, University of Kentucky, 1967.

**573.** McKenney, Thomas L. *Memoirs, Official and Personal.* With an Introduction by Herman J. Viola. Lincoln, Neb.: University of Nebraska Press, 1973 (originally published 1846). McKenney was the able superintendent of Indian Affairs under Calhoun as secretary of war.

**574.** Morse, Jedidiah. *A Report to the Secretary of War of the United States, on Indian Affairs, Comprising a Narrative of a Tour Performed in the Summer of 1820* . . . . New Haven, Conn.: S. Converse, 1822.

**575.** Parker, Thomas Valentine. *The Cherokee Indians, with Special Reference to Their Relations with the United States Government.* New York: Grafton Press, 1907.

**576.** Peake, Ora Brooks. *A History of the United States Indian Factory System, 1795–1822.* Denver: Sage Books, 1954. The always troublesome question of regulation of Indian trade.

**577.** Prucha, Francis Paul. *American Indian Policy in the Formative Years: the Indian Trade and Intercourse Acts, 1790–1834.* Cambridge, Mass.: Harvard University Press, 1962.

**578.** Schoolcraft, Henry R. *Narrative Journal of Travels through the Northwestern Regions of the United States . . . to the Sources of the Mississippi River . . . in . . . 1820.* Albany, N.Y.: E. & E. Hosford, 1821. Schoolcraft was a northwestern Indian agent close to Calhoun and an able and sympathetic observer of Indian life.

579. Viola, Herman J. *Thomas L. McKenney: Architect of America's Early Indian Policy, 1818–1830.* Chicago: Swallow Press, 1974.

## 5. Miscellany

580. Bell, John R. *The Journal of Captain John R. Bell, Journalist for the Stephen H. Long Expedition to the Rocky Mountains.* Edited by Harlin M. Fuller and LeRoy R. Hafen. Glendale, Cal.: Arthur H. Clark, 1957. Record of a Western exploring expedition commissioned by Secretary of War Calhoun.

581. Espy, James P. *Philosophy of Storms.* Boston: Little, Brown & Co., 1841. Pioneering meterological study drawn from data collections initiated by Secretary of War Calhoun.

582. Hill, Forrest G. *Roads, Rails and Waterways: The Army Engineers and Early Transportation.* Norman, Okla.: University of Oklahoma Press, 1957. The War Department's involvement in internal improvements during Calhoun's administration.

583. James, Edwin, ed. *Account of an Expedition from Pittsburgh to the Rocky Mountains, Performed in the Years 1819 and '20 . . . .* 3 vols. Philadelphia: Carey & Lea, 1822–1823.

584. Nichols, Roger L., and Patrick L. Halley. *Stephen Long and American Frontier Exploration.* Newark, Del.: University of Delaware Press, 1980.

## D. PRESIDENTIAL AND VICE PRESIDENTIAL CANDIDACY, 1822–1824

585. "Cassius." *An Examination of Mr. Calhoun's Economy and an Apology for Those Members of Congress Who Have Been Denounced as Radicals.* No publisher: 1823. Attack on Secretary of War Calhoun and defense of congressional followers of William H. Crawford.

586. Cumming, Joseph Bryan. "The Cumming-McDuffie Duels." *Georgia Historical Quarterly* 44 (March 1960): 18–40. Good account of the tragic encounters between George McDuffie and William Cumming which grew out of the Calhoun-Crawford political rivalry.

**587.** Cutler, E. Wayne. "William H. Crawford: A Contextual Biography." Ph.D. dissertation, University of Texas, 1971. Good on the different and competing forms of Republicanism.

**588.** [Dallas, George M.?] "John C. Calhoun." Philadelphia *Franklin Gazette,* March 14, March 18, April 11, May 16, May 22, May 30, June 11, June 27, July 11, 1822. An early, laudatory biography designed to promote Calhoun's presidential candidacy.

**589.** Dix, Morgan, ed. *Memoirs of John Adams Dix.* 2 vols. New York: Harper & Brothers, 1883. Insider recollections by a Calhoun supporter of his presidential and vice presidential candidacy (2:309–314).

**590.** Edgar, Walter B. "Adams, Calhoun, the Election of 1824, and their Relationship." M.A. thesis, University of South Carolina, 1967. Calhoun and John Quincy Adams—friendship turned to enmity.

**591.** Hay, Thomas R. "John C. Calhoun and the Presidential Campaign of 1824." *North Carolina Historical Review* 12 (January 1935): 20–44.

**592.** Hemphill, W. Edwin. Introduction to Hemphill, ed., *The Papers of John C. Calhoun,* vol. 7, *1822–1823,* pp. xi–liv. Columbia, S.C.: University of South Carolina Press, 1973. Examines the later part of Calhoun's administration of the War Department and his presidential candidacy.

**593.** ———. Introduction to Hemphill, ed., *The Papers of John C. Calhoun,* vol. 8, *1823–1824,* pp. xi–xlviii. Columbia, S.C.: University of South Carolina Press, 1975. Treats aspects of Calhoun's service in the Monroe cabinet and of the election of 1824.

**594.** ———. Introduction to Hemphill, ed., *The Papers of John C. Calhoun,* vol. 9, *1824–1825,* pp. xi–lxiii. Columbia, S.C.: University of South Carolina Press, 1976. Examines aspects of Calhoun's service in Monroe's cabinet and of the election of 1824.

**595.** [Jameson, J. Franklin, ed.] "Virgil Maxcy on Calhoun's Political Opinions and Prospects, 1823." *American Historical Review* 12 (April 1907): 600–601.

**596.** Klein, Philip S. *Pennsylvania Politics, 1817–1832: A Game Without Rules.* Philadelphia: Historical Society of Pennsylvania, 1940. A key state in which Calhoun's presidential campaign foundered.

**597.** [McDuffie, George.] "Carolina." *An Address to the Citizens of North-Carolina, on the Subject of the Presidential Election*. Raleigh, N.C.: Bell & Lawrence, [1823.] Advocates Calhoun's claims for the presidency.

**598.** [Maxcy, Virgil.] *An Address to the People of Maryland*. [No place: 1823]. Advocates Calhoun's claims to the presidency.

**599.** *Presidential Election*. [Richmond: 1823]. A sizable collection of newspaper essays by various persons advocating Calhoun's claims to the presidency.

**600.** Skeen, C. Edward. "Calhoun, Crawford, and the Politics of Retrenchment." *South Carolina Historical Magazine* 73 (July 1972): 141–155. Political rivalry between the secretary of war and the secretary of the treasury.

**601.** [Swift, Joseph G.] "A Citizen of New-York." *Measures, Not Men. Illustrated by Some Remarks upon the Public Conduct and Character of John C. Calhoun*. New York: E.B. Clayton, 1823. A defense of Calhoun as a presidential contender.

**602.** [Swift, Joseph G.] *The Memoirs of General Joseph Gardner Swift, LL.D., U.S.A., . . . 1800–1865*. Privately printed, 1890. Memoirs of a young Army officer close to Calhoun.

**603.** Wiltse, Charles M. "John C. Calhoun and the 'A.B. Plot.'" *Journal of Southern History* 13 (February 1947): 46–61. A forgotten political incident.

**604.** ———. "Some Reflections of Administrative History." *Public Administration Review* 12 (Spring 1952): 113–119. Some aspects of the Monroe cabinet and the Calhoun-Crawford rivalry.

## E. VICE PRESIDENT UNDER ADAMS AND JACKSON, 1825–1832

### 1. The Adams Administration, 1825–1829

**605.** Brown, Richard H. "The Missouri Crisis, Slavery, and the Politics of Jacksonianism." *South Atlantic Quarterly* 65 (Winter 1966): 55–72. Essential to understanding the position of the South, the formation of the Democratic party, and Calhoun in the 1820s.

**606.** Bruns, Roger. "John C. Calhoun—the Rip Rap Imbroglio, 1826." In Arthur M. Schlesinger Jr. and Bruns, eds., *Congress Investigates. A Documentary History, 1792–1974,* 1:481–588. New York: Chelsea House, 1975, 5 vols. Investigation of a controversy arising out of contract while Calhoun was secretary of war.

**607.** Ewing, Gretchen Garst. "Duff Green, John C. Calhoun, and the Election of 1828." *South Carolina Historical Magazine* 79 (April 1978): 126–137. How Calhoun united with the Jackson ticket as vice presidential candidate.

**608.** Hargreaves, Mary W.M. *The Presidency of John Quincy Adams.* Lawrence, Kan.: University Press of Kansas, 1985. A detailed and judicious study of the middle 1820s and its major political figures, including Calhoun.

**609.** Hatch, Louis Clinton. *A History of the Vice-Presidency of the United States.* New York: American Historical Society, 1934; reprint, Freeport, N.Y.: Greenwood Press, 1970. Slight in regard to Calhoun.

**610.** "Patrick Henry." *An Argument on the Powers, Duties, and Conduct of the Hon. John C. Calhoun, as Vice-President of the United States, and President of the Senate.* Washington: Peter Force, 1827. Attack on Calhoun by a John Quincy Adams partisan for tolerating anti-administration speeches in the Senate.

**611.** Remini, Robert V. *The Election of Andrew Jackson.* Philadelphia: J.B. Lippincott, 1963. Formation of the Democratic party in the 1820s told from Martin Van Buren's viewpoint.

**612.** U.S. House of Representatives. "Report of the Committee Appointed on the 29th Dec. 1826, on a Letter of John C. Calhoun, Vice-President of the United States, Asking an Investigation of His Conduct While Secretary of War. With Accompanying Documents." *House Report* No. 79, 19th Congress, 2nd Session. Washington: Gales and Seaton, 1827. Majority and minority reports on the investigation of the "Rip Rap" contract.

**613.** Wilson, Clyde N. Introduction to Wilson, ed., *The Papers of John C. Calhoun,* vol. 10, *1825–1829,* pp. xiii–xlvi. Columbia, S.C.: University of South Carolina Press, 1977. Examines Calhoun as vice president, his conflict with John Quincy Adams, and the early stages of nullification.

614. Young, Klyde, and Lamar Middleton. *Heirs Apparent. The Vice-Presidents of the United States.* New York: Prentice-Hall, 1948. Popular treatment (pp. 79–93).

## 2. The First Jackson Administration, 1829–1833

615. Bowers, Claude G. *Party Battles of the Jackson Period.* Boston and New York: Houghton Mifflin, 1922. Romanticized political history with Calhoun as a villain.

616. Burke, Pauline W. *Emily Donelson of Tennessee.* 2 vols. Richmond, Va.: Garrett & Massie, 1941. This biography of Andrew Jackson's niece contains much information about the "Peggy" Eaton affair and other aspects of Washington life in the Jackson administrations.

617. Hamilton, James A. *Reminiscences of James A. Hamilton of Men and Events at Home and Abroad.* New York: Scribner & Co., 1869. Memoirs of a minor New York politician who acted as Van Buren's catspaw during the Calhoun-Jackson controversy over the Seminole War.

618. Latner, Richard B. *The Presidency of Andrew Jackson: White House Politics 1829–1837.* Athens, Ga.: University of Georgia Press, 1979. A detailed political study, considerably more factual and even-handed in regard to Calhoun than most Jackson studies.

619. "Peggy O'Neal; or the Doom of the Republic." *Southern Review* 12 (January-April 1873): 213–231. Report of an interview with Calhoun on the Eaton affair many years after the event.

620. Remini, Robert V. *Martin Van Buren and the Making of the Democratic Party.* New York and London: Columbia University Press, 1951. Decidedly from Van Buren's viewpoint.

621. Stenberg, Richard R. "Jackson's 'Rhea Letter' Hoax." *Journal of Southern History* 2 (1936): 480–496. Flaws in Jackson's position in the Seminole War controversy.

622. ———. "A Note on the Jackson-Calhoun Breach of 1830–1831." *Tyler's Historical Magazine* 21 (1939): 65–69.

## F. THE NULLIFICATION EPISODE, 1828–1833

### 1. Documents

**623.** Ames, Herman V., ed. *State Documents on Federal Relations: the States and the United States*, 6 vols. Philadelphia: 1900–1906. Prints basic public documents from the nullification controversy.

**624.** Cooper, Thomas. *Lectures on the Elements of Political Economy.* Columbia, S.C.: M'Morris & Wilson, 1829; London: R. Hunter, 1831. Free trade argument by a South Carolina militant.

**625.** Freehling, William W., ed. *The Nullification Era: A Documentary Record.* New York: Harper & Row, 1967. A slight collection designed to support the thesis of #656.

**626.** Public letters to Calhoun from William Henry Harrison, November 29, 1831–April 30, 1832 (five letters). Cincinnati, Ohio, *Daily Gazette*, December 13 and December 21, 1831, January 26, May 19, and May 26, 1832. The former general and senator from Ohio and future president challenges Calhoun on the tariff.

**627.** *The Report, Ordinance, and Addresses of the Convention of the People of South Carolina, Adopted November 24, 1832.* Columbia, S.C.: A.S. Johnston, 1832. Official proceedings of the South Carolina nullification convention.

**628.** Rabun, James, ed. "Documents Illustrating the Development of the Doctrine of Interposition, 1790–1832." *Journal of Public Law* 5 (Spring 1956): 49–89.

**629.** Romaine, Benjamin. *State Sovereignty, and a Certain Dissolution of the Union. To the Honorable John C. Calhoun, Now Vice-President of the United States.* New York: J. Kenneday, 1832. Anti-nullification.

**630.** [Turnbull, Robert J.] "Brutus." *The Crisis.* Charleston, S.C.: A.E. Miller, 1827. Influential pamphlet in developing anti-tariff and nullification opinion in South Carolina.

### 2. Nullification as Doctrine

**631.** Corwin, Edwin S. "National Power and State Interposition, 1787–1861." *Michigan Law Review* 10 (May 1912): 535–551.

**632.** Denny, William H. "South Carolina's Conception of the Union in 1832." *South Carolina Historical Magazine* 78 (July 1977): 171–183.

**633.** Ellis, Richard F. *The Union: Jacksonian Democracy, States' Rights and the Nullification Crisis.* New York: Oxford University Press, 1987. Nullification as a conflict between different schools of states' rights advocates.

**634.** Green, Benjamin E. "Calhoun—Nullification Explained." *Southern Historical Society Papers* 14 (1886): 226–241. Sympathetic exposition by a follower.

**635.** Green, Fletcher M. "Calhoun's Exposition." In *Dictionary of American History,* 5 vols. Edited by James Truslow Adams. New York: Charles Scribner's Sons, 1940, 1:269.

**636.** ———. "Nullification." In *Dictionary of American History,* 5 vols. Edited by James Truslow Adams. New York: Charles Scribner's Sons, 1940, 4:153–154.

**637.** McCoy, Drew R. *The Last of the Fathers: James Madison and the Republican Legacy.* Cambridge, Mass.: Cambridge University Press, 1989. The elderly Madison's critical but somewhat ambivalent reaction to the nullification movement.

**638.** McLaughlin, Andrew C. "Social Compact and Constitutional Construction." *American Historical Review* 5 (April 1900): 467–490. Both sides in the nullification controversy followed social compact theory.

**639.** Matthews, Steve A. "The Political Understanding of William Harper." In *South Carolina Legal History.* Edited by Herbert A. Johnson, pp. 119–129. Spartanburg, S.C.: Reprint Co., 1980. The thoughts of a South Carolina jurist and defender of nullification.

**640.** Miles, Edwin A. "After John Marshall's Decision: *Worcester v. Georgia* and the Nullification Crisis." *Journal of Southern History* 39 (1973): 519–544. Georgia's contemporary "nullification" of federal Indian treaties.

**641.** Miller, Arthur S., and Ronald Howell. "Interposition, Nullification, and the Delicate Division of Power in a Federal System." *Journal of Public Law* 5 (Spring 1956): 2–48.

642. Morse, Howard N. "Doctrines of Nullification and Secession—A Historical Study." *South Carolina Law Quarterly* 2 (September 1949): 245–264.

643. Nagel, Paul C. *One Nation Indivisible: The Union in American Thought, 1776–1861*. New York: Oxford University Press, 1964. Study of the ideas of "union" and "disunion."

644. Stampp, Kenneth M. "The Concept of a Perpetual Union." *Journal of American History* 65 (June 1978): 5–33. On the tradition-breaking nature of Jackson's response to nullification.

645. Weaver, Richard M. "Two Orators." *Modern Age* 14 (Summer-Fall 1970): 226–241. Profound analysis of the differing views of the American tradition at stake in the Webster-Hayne debate.

646. Wilson, Major L. "'Liberty and Union': An Analysis of Three Concepts Involved in the Nullification Controversy." *Journal of Southern History* 33 (August 1967): 331–355. The controversy involved three, rather than two, competing concepts of the Union.

647. ———. *Space, Time, and Freedom: The Quest for Nationality and the Irrepressible Conflict, 1815–1861*. Westport, Conn.: Greenwood Press, 1974. Imaginative exploration of the issues involved in state-federal conflict.

## 3. Nullification as Historical Episode

648. Bancroft, Frederic. *Calhoun and the South Carolina Nullification Movement*. Baltimore: The Johns Hopkins Press, 1928. Outdated.

649. Bergeron, Paul H. "The Nullification Controversy Revisited." *Tennessee Historical Quarterly* 35 (Fall 1976): 263–275. Criticism of Freehling's view (#656) that slavery rather than the tariff motivated nullification.

650. ———. "Tennessee's Response to the Nullification Crisis." *Journal of Southern History* 39 (February 1973): 23–44. Unfriendly response to South Carolina's actions in another Southern state.

651. Boucher, Chauncey S. *The Nullification Controversy in South Carolina*. Chicago: University of Chicago Press, 1916. Outdated.

652. Brasington, George F. "Jackson, Calhoun, and State Rights." *Emory University Quarterly* 15 (October 1959): 168–175. Calhoun and Jackson were both advocates of state rights, but were forced into conflict by different situations.

653. Bridgeforth, Lucie Robertson. "Mississippi's Response to Nullification, 1833." *Journal of Mississippi History* 45 (February 1983): 1–22.

654. Capers, Gerald M. "A Reconsideration of John C. Calhoun's Transition from Nationalism to Nullification." *Journal of Southern History* 14 (February 1948): 34–48. Attributes Calhoun's actions to opportunism.

655. Coulter, E. Merton, "The Nullification Movement in Georgia." *Georgia Historical Quarterly* 5 (March 1921): 3–39. Study of the failure of the nullification movement in another state.

656. Freehling, William W. *Prelude to Civil War: The Nullification Controversy in South Carolina, 1816–1836*. New York: Harper & Row, 1965. Sees nullification as related less to the tariff than to slavery tensions.

657. Green, Fletcher M. "Tariff of Abominations (1828)." In *Dictionary of American History*, 5 vols. Edited by James Truslow Adams. New York: Charles Scribner's Sons, 1940, 5:223–224.

658. ———. "Webster-Hayne Debate." In *Dictionary of American History*, 5 vols. Edited by James Truslow Adams. New York: Charles Scribner's Sons, 1940, 5:431–432.

659. Hearon, Cleo. "Nullification in Mississippi." In *Mississippi Historical Society Publications* 12 (1912): 137–171.

660. Houston, David F. *A Critical Study of Nullification in South Carolina*. New York: Longmans, Green and Co., 1896. Outdated.

661. Latner, Richard B. "The Nullification Crisis and Republican Subversion." *Journal of Southern History* 43 (1977): 19–38. Describes Andrew Jackson's view.

662. Maier, Pauline. "The Road Not Taken: Nullification, John C. Calhoun, and the Revolutionary Tradition in South Carolina." *South Carolina Historical Magazine* 82 (January 1981): 1–19. The eighteenth-century roots of South Carolina actions.

663. Ochenkowski, John Paul. "The Origins of Nullification in South Carolina." *South Carolina Historical Magazine* 83 (April 1982): 121–153. Electoral analysis.

664. Pease, Jane H., and William Pease. "The Economics and Politics of Charleston's Nullification Crisis." *Journal of Southern History* 47 (November 1981): 335–362.

665. Peterson, Merrill D. *Olive Branch and Sword: The Compromise of 1833*. Baton Rouge, La.: Louisiana State University Press, 1982. Detailed study of the resolution of the nullification crisis.

666. Rell, Carl Lewis. "A Rhetorical History of James Hamilton, Jr.; the Nullification Era in South Carolina." Ph.D. dissertation, University of Kansas, 1971. Hamilton was the fiery governor and grass-roots leader of the "nullification" movement.

667. Rogers, George C. "South Carolina Federalists and the Origins of the Nullification Movement." *South Carolina Historical Magazine* 71 (1970): 17–32. Attainment of internal unity in South Carolina as a prelude to nullification.

668. Stanwood, Edward. *American Tariff Controversies in the Nineteenth Century*, 2 vols. Boston and New York: 1903. Standard study.

669. Stenberg, Richard R. "The Jefferson Birthday Dinner, 1830." *Journal of Southern History* 4 (1938): 334–346. The celebrated Calhoun-Jackson clash of toasts.

670. Stewart, James Brewer. "A Great Talking and Eating Machine: Patriarchy, Mobilization and the Dynamics of Nullification in South Carolina." *Civil War History* 37 (September 1981): 197–220.

671. Wilson, Clyde N. Introduction to Wilson, ed., *The Papers of John C. Calhoun*, vol 11, *1829–1832*, pp. xiii–xxxix. Columbia, S.C.: University of South Carolina Press, 1978. Elucidates Calhoun's relationship with Andrew Jackson and nullification.

672. ———. "John C. Calhoun and the Nullification Conflict." In *Book of Days 1987. An Encyclopedia of Information Sources on Historical Figures and Events*, pp. 651–652. Ann Arbor, Mich.: Pierian Press, 1986. Narrative and bibliography of the most dramatic episode of Calhoun's career.

**673.** Wiltse, Charles M. "Calhoun and Nullification." In *The American Story: The Age of Exploration to the Age of the Atom*, pp. 174–178. Edited by Earl Schenck Miers. New York: Channel Press, 1956.

## G. SENATOR, 1833–1843

### 1. General

**674.** Brown, Thomas, "Southern Whigs and the Politics of Statesmanship, 1833–1841." *Journal of Southern History* 46 (August 1980): 361–380. Brief though suggestive effort to understand the motives of Calhoun's main opponents within the South.

**675.** Fisher, John E. "The Dilemma of a States' Rights Whig: The Congressional Career of R.M.T. Hunter, 1837–1841." *Virginia Magazine of History and Biography* 81 (October 1973): 387–404. Uncertain party alliances that affected many of Calhoun's followers.

**676.** Harwell, Donald Ray. "The State Rights Faction of the Twenty-Sixth Congress, 1839–1840." M.A. thesis, Vanderbilt University, 1980. A study of the movement of Calhoun supporters back into the Democratic party.

**677.** James, Marquis. *Andrew Jackson: Portrait of a President*. Indianapolis and New York: Bobbs-Merrill, 1937. Vivid and popular pro-Jackson treatment of the period.

**678.** "Political Portraits with Pen and Pencil (No. V): John C. Calhoun." *United States Magazine and Democratic Review* 2 (April 1838): 64–84. Assessment of Calhoun's relationship to the Democratic party at this time.

**679.** Schlesinger, Arthur M., Jr. *The Age of Jackson*. Boston: Little, Brown & Co., 1945. Classic, controversial interpretation of Jacksonian democracy, valuable for Calhoun chiefly for interesting but undeveloped suggestions about his mutually sympathetic relationship with the radical Democrats of New York.

**680.** Wilson, Clyde N. Introduction to Wilson, ed., *The Papers of John C. Calhoun*, vol. 13, *1835–1837*, pp. ix–xxii. Columbia, S.C.: University of South Carolina Press, 1980. Examines Calhoun's political thought and strategy in the post-nullification period.

**681.** ——. Introduction to Wilson, ed., *The Papers of John C. Calhoun,* vol. 15, *1839–1841,* pp. ix–xxii. Columbia, S.C.: University of South Carolina Press, 1983. Analyzes Calhoun's political strategy in his 1839 reunion with Martin Van Buren and in the election of 1840.

**682.** Wilson, Major L. *The Presidency of Martin Van Buren.* Lawrence, Kan.: University Press of Kansas, 1984. Excellent on Calhoun's national role in the later 1830s.

**683.** ——. "Republicanism and the Idea of Party in the Jacksonian Period." *Journal of the Early Republic.* 8 (Winter 1988): 419–442. Indispensable for sorting out the difference between Democrats and Whigs.

## 2. National Issues

**684.** Bourne, Edward G. *The History of the Surplus Revenue of 1837.* New York and London: Putnam's, 1885. Standard study of a major congressional issue.

**685.** Eichert, Magdalen. "A Consideration of the Interests which Lay Behind the Attitudes of Benton, Clay, Webster, and Calhoun in the Development of Public Land Policy, 1830–1841." Ph.D. dissertation, New York University, 1950. Systematic exposition of an important congressional issue.

**686.** ——. "John C. Calhoun's Land Policy of Cession." *South Carolina Historical Magazine* 55 (October 1954): 198–209. Examination of an important and little-known facet of Calhoun's political program—the cession of public lands to the Western states.

**687.** Gordon, Armistead C. *William Fitzhugh Gordon, A Virginian of the Old School: His Life, Times, and Contemporaries (1787–1858).* New York: Neale Publishing Co., 1909. Material on Calhoun and the Subtreasury in this biography of a Virginia congressman.

**688.** Hammond, Bray. *Banks and Politics in America: From the Revolution to the Civil War.* Princeton, N.J.: Princeton University Press, 1957. Calhoun's views on banking and currency and his role in the Jackson bank war.

**689.** Lester, C. Edwards. *The Glory and the Shame of England.* 2 vols. New York: Harper & Brothers, 1842. Includes an essay addressed to Calhoun on the oppressive post-emancipation labor practices in British colonies.

**690.** "Lowndes" (pseudonym). *The Letters of Lowndes, Addressed to the Hon. John C. Calhoun.* New York: D. Appleton & Co., and Philadelphia: Geo. S. Appleton, 1843. An elaborate essay by a Northern Whig, attacking Calhoun's career, especially in regard to banking issues.

**691.** McGrane, Reginald C. *The Panic of 1837: Some Financial Problems of the Jacksonian Era.* Chicago: University of Chicago Press, 1924.

**692.** Merriman, John. "Scenes from a Marriage. Makeup or Breakup: John C. Calhoun, Internal Improvements, and the Federal Compact." Unpublished paper, Emory University, 1988.

**693.** Parish, John Carl. *George Wallace Jones.* Iowa City: State Historical Society of Iowa, 1912. Calhoun's conversations on freesoilism with a major early leader of Iowa.

**694.** Wilson, Clyde N. "John C. Calhoun and Antebellum America." In *The David A. Sayre History Symposium: Collected Lectures, 1985-1989.* Edited by F. Kevin Simon. Lexington, Ky.: Sayre School, 1990. Calhoun's neglected importance in regard to the banking, public lands, and Oregon issues in the 1830s and 1840s.

### 3. South Carolina Politics in the Post-Nullification Period

**695.** Derrick, Samuel M. *Centennial History of the South Carolina Railroad.* Columbia, S.C.: The State Co., 1930; reprint, Spartanburg, S.C.: Reprint Co., 1975. The South Carolina Railroad was a large and controversial issue in the 1830s.

**696.** Lander, Ernest M. "The Calhoun-Preston Feud, 1836-1842." *South Carolina Historical Magazine* 59 (1958): 24-37. Whiggish unrest against Calhoun at home.

**697.** Richards, Miles S. "Pierce Mason Butler: The South Carolina Years, 1830-1841." *South Carolina Historical Magazine* 87 (January 1986): 14-29. Butler was governor of South Carolina during 1836-1838 and a member of the William C. Preston Whig faction opposed to Calhoun.

**698.** ———. "The South Carolina General Assembly after Nullification." M.A. thesis, University of South Carolina, 1988. The internal workings of the legislature which followed Calhoun's lead on federal affairs and repeatedly re-elected him as U.S. Senator with near unanimity.

**699.** Rogers, George C., Jr. "Henry Laurens Pinckney: Thoughts on His Career." In *South Carolina Journals and Journalists*. Edited by James B. Meriwether, pp. 163–172. Spartanburg, S.C.: Reprint Co., 1975. A Charleston congressman and editor differs with Calhoun during the 1830s.

**700.** Schultz, Charles R. "Hayne's Magnificent Dream: Factors Which Influenced Efforts to Join Cincinnati and Charleston by Railroad, 1835–1860." Ph.D. dissertation, Ohio State University, 1966.

## H. PRESIDENTIAL CANDIDACY, 1842–1844

**701.** Brownson, Orestes A. "Mr. Calhoun and the Baltimore Convention." *Brownson's Quarterly Review* 1 (April 1844): 257–269. Calhoun's candidacy supported by a Northern admirer.

**702.** *The Calhoun Textbook*. New York: Herald Office, [1843]. Collection of press encomiums published by Calhoun's supporters in New York City.

**703.** *Democratic Republican Mass Meeting of Electors of Michigan Friendly to the Nomination of John C. Calhoun*. [Detroit: 1843.] Support for Calhoun's candidacy, signed by more than 600 voters.

**704.** Fitzsimmons, Matthew A. "Calhoun's Bid for the Presidency, 1841–1844." *Mississippi Valley Historical Review* 38 (June 1951): 39–60. Calhoun's candidacy failed, but killed off Van Buren and prepared the way for Polk.

**705.** Lambert, Oscar Doane. *Presidential Politics in the United States, 1841–1844*. Durham, N.C.: Duke University Press, 1936. Slight on Calhoun.

**706.** [Maxcy, Virgil.] *Democratic National Convention*. [New York: 1843]. Calhoun campaign pamphlet for distribution at state conventions.

**707.** New York *Evening Post*, September 1843. Interesting accounts of the activities of Calhoun's supporters in New York City.

**708.** "Political Portraits with Pen and Pencil (No. XXXVI), John C. Calhoun of South Carolina." *United States Magazine and Democratic Review* 12 (January 1843): 93–95. Discussion of Calhoun's relation to the Democratic party.

**709.** *Proceedings of the Democratic State Convention, Composed of Delegates from the Several Districts and Parishes of the State of South-Carolina, Assembled at Columbia, on the 22nd of May, 1843.* Columbia, S.C.: printed at the South Carolinian Office, 1843. Calhoun's platform for the Democratic presidential nomination.

**710.** [Rhett, Robert Barnwell.] *An Appeal to the Democratic Party, on the Principles of a National Convention for the Nomination of President and Vice-President of the United States.* [No place: 1843]. Sets forth position of supporters of Calhoun's presidential candidacy on rules of representation and the process of electing delegates to the Democratic National Convention.

**711.** [Rhett, Robert Barnwell.] *The Compromises of the Constitution Considered in the Organization of a National Convention*. [Washington?: 1843] Argument of Calhoun supporters on the manner of apportioning delegates.

**712.** Wilson, Clyde N. Introduction to Wilson, ed., *The Papers of John C. Calhoun*, vol. 17, *1843–1844*, pp. ix–xxvii. Columbia, S.C.: University of South Carolina Press, 1986. Aspects of Calhoun's presidential candidacy and withdrawal.

## L. SECRETARY OF STATE, 1844–1845

### 1. The Tyler Administration

**713.** Chitwood, Oliver Perry. *John Tyler: Champion of the Old South.* New York and London: D. Appleton-Century, 1939. Standard and sympathetic biography.

**714.** Morgan, Robert J. *A Whig Embattled: The Presidency under John Tyler.* Lincoln, Neb.: University of Nebraska Press, 1954. Superficial political history.

**715.** Peterson, Norma Lois. *The Presidencies of William Henry Harrison and John Tyler.* Lawrence, Kan.: University Press of Kansas, 1989. Another good, balanced and detailed study in the "American Presidency" series.

**716.** Seager, Robert, II. *And Tyler Too: A Biography of John and Julia Gardiner Tyler.* New York: McGraw-Hill, 1963. Vivid, with much human interest.

**717.** Wise, Henry A. *Seven Decades of the Union.* Philadelphia: J.B. Lippincott, 1881. Memoirs of the Tyler administration's leader in the House of Representatives.

**2. The State Department and Diplomacy**

**718.** Adams, Randolph G. "Abel Parker Upshur." In *The American Secretaries of State and Their Diplomacy.* Edited by Samuel F. Bemis, 5:65–124. New York: Alfred A. Knopf, 1928. Calhoun's immediate predecessor and close collaborator.

**719.** Bailey, Thomas A. *A Diplomatic History of the American People.* New York: Appleton-Century-Crofts, 1950 (and many later editions). This standard textbook has next to nothing on Calhoun.

**720.** Bemis, Samuel F. *Diplomatic History of the United States.* New York: Henry Holt, 1936 (and many later editions). A quite brief but balanced treatment of Calhoun in the State Department.

**721.** Brauer, Kinley. "The Great American Desert Revisited: Recent Literature and Prospects for the Study of American Foreign Relations, 1815–1861." *Diplomatic History* 13 (Summer 1989): 395–417. Good historiographical discussion of writings on the middle period of American diplomacy and the lacunae in them.

**722.** Frothingham, Paul Revere. *Edward Everett: Orator and Statesman.* Boston: Houghton Mifflin, 1925. The U.S. minister to Great Britain during Calhoun's tenure.

**723.** Garrison, George Pierce. *Westward Extension, 1841–1850* (Vol. 17 of *The American Nation: A History*). New York and London:

Harper and Brothers, 1906. Solid standard survey of the era of expansion.

**724.** Graebner, Norman A., ed. *Ideas and Diplomacy: Readings in the Intellectual Tradition of American Foreign Policy.* Edited with a commentary. New York: Oxford University Press, 1964. The Great Triumvirate as a conservative counter-weight to Jacksonian jingoism, the best brief treatment of Calhoun's foreign policy.

**725.** Gujer, Bruno. "Free Trade and Slavery: Calhoun's Defense of Southern Interests Against British Interference, 1811–1848." Ph.D. dissertation, University of Zurich, 1971. Detailed study of Calhoun's foreign policy.

**726.** Jones, Wilbur Devereux. *The American Problem in British Diplomacy, 1841–1861.* Athens, Ga.: University of Georgia Press, 1974.

**727.** Reeves, Jesse Slidell. *American Diplomacy under Tyler and Polk.* Baltimore: Johns Hopkins Press, 1907; reprint, Gloucester, Mass.: Peter Smith, 1967. Deals only with the major issues of Texas and Oregon and that uninspiredly.

**728.** Sioussat, St. George L. "John Caldwell Calhoun." In Samuel F. Bemis, ed., *The American Secretaries of State and Their Diplomacy,* 5:125–233. New York: Alfred A. Knopf, 1928. New York: Cooper Square Publishers, 1963. Standard overview.

**729.** Wilson, Clyde N. Introduction to Wilson, ed., *The Papers of John C. Calhoun,* vol. 18, *1844,* pp. ix–xxviii. Columbia, S.C.: University of South Carolina Press, 1989. Calhoun's administration of the State Department.

**730.** ———. "Robert Greenhow." In *American Historians, 1607–1865,* ed. by Wilson (Vol. 30 of *Dictionary of Literary Biography*), pp. 102–107. Detroit: Gale Research Co., 1984. Greenhow was chief translator and librarian of the State Department when Calhoun was secretary.

## 3. Texas and Slavery

**731.** Adams, Ephraim D. *British Interests and Activities in Texas, 1838–1846.* Baltimore: Johns Hopkins Press, 1910.

**732.** Boucher, Chauncey S. "The Annexation of Texas and the Bluffton Movement in South Carolina." *Mississippi Valley Historical Review* 6 (1919): 3–33. Rebellion of South Carolina secessionists against Calhoun.

**733.** Crallé, Richard K. "Correspondence in Relation to the Annexation of Texas. Preliminary Remarks." In Crallé, ed., *The Works of John C. Calhoun,* 5:311–320. (See #219.) The question of Texas annexation examined by Calhoun's chief clerk at the time he was secretary of state.

**734.** "The Democratic Review and Mr. Calhoun." *United States Magazine and Democratic Review* 16 (February 1845): 107–108. Attack on Calhoun as secretary of state by Northern Democrats.

**735.** [Hammond, Jabez D.] "Hamden." *Letter to the Hon. John C. Calhoun, on the Annexation of Texas.* Cooperstown, N.Y.: H. & E. Phinney, 1844. Criticism of the annexation of Texas by a New York Free Soiler.

**736.** [Janney, Samuel M.?] "A Virginian." *Letter Addressed to the Hon. John C. Calhoun. On the Law Relating to Slaves, Free Negroes and Mulattoes.* Washington: J. and G.S. Gideon, 1845. Mild criticism of Calhoun's defense of slavery.

**737.** Jollivet, Adolphe. *Documents américains, annexion du Texas, emancipation des Noirs, Politique de l'Angleterre.* Paris: de l'Imprimerie de Bruneau, 1845. Argument against British abolitionist influence by the leading defender of French colonial slavery, based upon Calhoun's arguments.

**738.** Merk, Frederick. *Slavery and the Annexation of Texas.* New York: Alfred A. Knopf, 1972. Standard study arguing the thesis that territorial expansion was motivated by slavery.

**739.** Norwood, John Nelson. *The Schism in the Methodist Episcopal Church, 1844: A Study in Ecclesiastical Politics.* In *Alfred University Studies* 1 (1923). Calhoun and the Southern Methodist ministry against abolitionism.

**740.** Pletcher, David A. *The Diplomacy of Annexation: Texas, Oregon, and the Mexican War.* Columbia: University of Missouri Press, 1973. Detailed study, both for Calhoun's State Department period and the period following in the Senate.

**741.** Silverthorne, Elizabeth. *Ashbel Smith of Texas.* College Station, Tex.: Texas A & M Press, 1982. Extensive material on collaboration between Calhoun and Smith, leading diplomat of the Texas Republic in Europe.

**742.** Smith, Ashbel. *Reminiscences of the Texas Republic.* Galveston, Tex.: Galveston Historical Society, 1876. Memoirs of a Texas Republic diplomat closely allied with Calhoun.

**743.** Smith, Justin H. *The Annexation of Texas.* New York: Macmillan, 1911. Old standard, somewhat influenced by the slave power conspiracy idea.

**744.** Smither, Harriet. "English Abolitionists and the Annexation of Texas." *Southwestern Historical Quarterly* 32 (January 1929): 193–205. A spur to annexation sentiment in Texas and the U.S.

**745.** Soulsby, Hugh G. *The Right of Search and the Slave Trade in Anglo-American Relations, 1814–1862.* Baltimore: Johns Hopkins Press, 1933.

**746.** Walker, Robert J. "Memoranda" [of interview with Calhoun], December 1844. In *Letters and Times of the Tylers.* Edited by Lyon G. Tyler, 3:152. (See #166.) Consultation between Secretary of State Calhoun and a leading Texas annexationist in the Senate over strategy.

**747.** Wilkins, Joe B. "Window on Freedom: The South's Response to the Emancipation of the Slaves in the British West Indies, 1833–1861." Ph.D. dissertation, University of South Carolina, 1977. Calhoun on slavery and emancipation in the Caribbean.

**748.** Wilson, Clyde N. Introduction to Wilson, ed., *The Papers of John C. Calhoun,* vol. 19, *1844,* pp. ix–xxii. Columbia, S.C.: University of South Carolina Press, 1990. Calhoun's strategy in regard to British antislavery influence in the New World.

**749.** ———. Introduction to Wilson, ed., *The Papers of John C. Calhoun,* vol. 20, *1844.* Columbia: University of South Carolina Press, in press. Aspects of Calhoun's administration of the State Department, the Texas annexation question, and the "Bluffton movement."

## 4. Other Issues

**750.** Boyd, Jesse W. "Lopez's Expedition to Cuba." *Gulf States Historical Magazine* 2 (March-May 1904): 329–330. Some near contemporary recollections concerning Calhoun's views on the U.S. relationship to Cuba.

751. Corbett, Percy E. *The Settlement of Canadian-American Disputes*. New Haven, Conn.: Yale University Press, 1937.

752. Crallé, Richard K. "The Oregon Negotiation." In Crallé, ed., *The Works of John C. Calhoun*, 5:414–415. (See #219.) Calhoun's role in the settlement of the Oregon question examined by his chief assistant as secretary of state.

753. Greenhow, Robert. *The History of Oregon and California, and the Other Territories on the North-West Coast of North America*. London: J. Murray, and Boston: C.C. Little & James Brown, 1844. Unofficial presentation of the American position on Oregon by one of Calhoun's subordinates in the State Department.

754. Henderson, William O. *The Zollverein*. London: Frank Cass, 1959.

755. Hill, Lawrence F. *Diplomatic Relations Between the United States and Brazil*. Durham, N.C.: Duke University Press, 1932.

756. Meyer, Isidore S., ed. *Early History of Zionism in America*. New York: Arno Press, 1977. Failed attempt to establish a U.S. Consulate in Jerusalem, 1844.

757. Parks, E. Taylor. *Colombia and the United States*. Durham, N.C.: Duke University Press, 1935.

758. Schafer, Joseph, "The British Attitude toward the Oregon Question, 1815–1846." *American Historical Review* 16 (January 1911): 273–299.

759. Stevens, Sylvester K. *American Expansion in Hawaii, 1842–1898*. Harrisburg, Pa.: Archives Publishing Co., 1945.

760. Tansill, Charles C. *The United States and Santo Domingo, 1798–1873*. Baltimore: Johns Hopkins Press, 1938.

761. Wilson, Clyde N. "Beyond Texas and Oregon: John C. Calhoun and the Global Expansion of the United States." Unpublished paper presented to the Society of Historians of American Foreign Relations, Williamsburg, Va., June 1989. Some neglected aspects of the world-

## J. SENATOR, 1845–1850

### 1. General

**762.** Bergeron, Paul H. *The Presidency of James K. Polk.* Lawrence, Kan.: University Press of Kansas, 1987. Another good political survey in the "American Presidency" series.

**763.** Curti, Merle. *The American Peace Crusade, 1815–1860.* Durham, N.C.: Duke University Press, 1929. Pacifist approval of Calhoun's role in the Oregon crisis.

**764.** Ellison, William H., ed. "Memoir of William M. Gwin." *California Historical Society Quarterly* 19 (1940): 1–26, 157–184, 256–277, 344–367. Calhoun's interest in the Pacific region as seen by an early California senator.

**765.** Fulkerson, H.S. *Random Recollections of Early Days in Mississippi.* Baton Rouge, La.: Otto Claitor, 1972; reprint of 1885 edition. Chapter 7 contains first-hand recollections of Calhoun's visit to the Southwest in late 1845.

**766.** Graebner, Norman A. *Empire on the Pacific: A Study in American Continental Expansion.* New York: Ronald Press, 1955. Good discussion of Calhoun's relation to the Oregon issue in the Senate.

**767.** ———. *Foundations of American Foreign Policy: A Realist Appraisal from Franklin to McKinley.* Wilmington, Del.: Scholarly Resources, 1985. Good though brief discussion of Calhoun's relation to the Mexican War.

**768.** Lander, Ernest M. *Reluctant Imperialists: Calhoun, the South Carolinians, and the Mexican War.* Baton Rouge, La., and London: Louisiana State University Press, 1980. Revises the common theory that South Carolinians were eager for territorial expansion.

**769.** Rayback, Joseph G. "Presidential Ambitions of John C. Calhoun, 1844–1848." *Journal of Southern History* 14 (August 1948): 331–356. Superficial and exaggerated argument for Calhoun's burning ambition in his last years.

**770.** Walmsley, James E. "The Return of John C. Calhoun to the Senate in 1845." In *American Historical Association Annual Report* for 1913, 1:159–165. Washington: U.S. Government Printing Office, 1915, 2 vols. Descriptive.

## 2. The Crisis of 1850 and Its Aftermath

**771.** Ames, Herman V. "John C. Calhoun and the Secession Movement of 1850." *American Antiquarian Society Proceedings,* new series 28 (1918): 19.

**772.** Barnwell, John. *Love of Order: South Carolina's First Secession Crisis.* Chapel Hill, N.C.: University of North Carolina Press, 1982. South Carolina politics in the immediate post-Calhoun era.

**773.** Boucher, Chauncey S. "The Secession and Cooperation Movements in South Carolina, 1848–1852." In *Washington University Studies* 5 (April 1918): 67–138. Division between immediate secessionists and co-operationists who wanted to wait for other states.

**774.** Breese, Donald H. "James L. Orr, Calhoun, and the Cooperationist Tradition in South Carolina." *South Carolina Historical Magazine* 80 (October 1979): 273–285. Study of the South Carolinians who followed Calhoun after his death in supporting Southern cooperation over secession.

**775.** Fehrenbacher, Don E. *The Dred Scott Case: Its Significance in American Law and Politics.* New York: Oxford University Press, 1978. Calhoun on the issue of slavery in the territories.

**776.** Fisher, George P. "Webster and Calhoun in the Debate of 1850." *Scribners' Magazine* 37 (May 1905): 578–586. Descriptive.

**777.** Green, Fletcher M. "Address of the Southern Delegates." In *Dictionary of American History,* 5 vols. Edited by James Truslow Adams. New York: Charles Scribner's Sons, 1940, 1:10. Calhoun's only partially successful effort to achieve Southern unity in Congress.

**778.** ———. "The Tarpley Letter (July 9, 1849)." In *Dictionary of American History,* 5 vols. Edited by James Truslow Adams. New York: Charles Scribner's Sons, 1940, 5:224. After his death Calhoun's letter to a Mississippi politician became part of a controversy over Southern strategy and whether he recommended secession.

779. Hamer, Philip M. *The Secession Movement in South Carolina, 1847–1852*. Allentown, Pa.: H. Ray Haas & Co., 1918.

780. Hamilton, Holman. *Prologue to Conflict: The Crisis and Compromise of 1850*. Lexington, Ky.: University of Kentucky Press, 1964. Standard study.

781. Hilliard, Henry W. *Politics and Pen Pictures at Home and Abroad*. New York: G.P. Putnam, 1892. Firsthand account of Calhoun's last days in the Senate by an Alabama politician.

782. Jennings, Thelma. *The Nashville Convention: Southern Movement for Unity, 1848–1850*. Memphis, Tenn.: Memphis State University Press, 1980. Efforts at Southern unity.

783. Johnson, Ludwell H. *Division and Reunion: America, 1848–1877*. New York: John Wiley & Sons, 1978. Early chapters survey Calhoun's last years.

784. Parrish, William E. *David Rice Atchison of Missouri, Border Politician*. Columbia: University of Missouri Press, 1961. Senator Atchison was a close associate and follower of Calhoun in his last years.

785. Potter, David M. *The Impending Crisis, 1848–1861*. New York: Harper & Row, 1976. Classic study of the prewar period.

786. Roback, Jennifer. *An Imaginary Negro in an Impossible Place: The Territories and Secession*. Princeton, N.J.: Princeton University Press, in press. An original interpretation of the conflict over slavery in the territories from a "public choice" and "common property" perspective.

787. Russell, Robert R. "Constitutional Doctrines in Regard to Slavery in the Territories." *Journal of Southern History*. 32 (1966): 466–486. Good exposition of Calhoun's and competing views.

788. Schultz, Harold S. *Nationalism and Sectionalism in South Carolina, 1852–1860: A Study of the Movement for Southern Independence*. Durham, N.C.: Duke University Press, 1950. Classic study of the different factions and gradations of opinion in South Carolina on secession.

789. Silbey, Joel H. "John C. Calhoun and the Limits of Southern Congressional Unity, 1841–1850." *The Historian* 30 (November 1967):

58–71. Calhoun's limited success in overcoming party loyalty and achieving sectional unity among Southern congressmen.

**790.** Tozawa, Kenji. ["John C. Calhoun and the 1850 Compromise."] *Ehime Law Journal* 13 (March 1987): 159–206. Japanese study.

## 3. Selected Memorials

**791.** Campbell, John A. *An Address upon the Life and Public Services of John C. Calhoun.* Mobile, Ala.: Dade, Thompson & Co., 1851. Campbell was an Alabama political leader and U.S. Supreme Court justice.

**792.** Henry, Robert. *Eulogy on the Late Honorable John Caldwell Calhoun, delivered at Columbia, South Carolina, on Thursday, May 16, 1850.* Columbia, S.C.: I.C. Morgan, 1851. Henry was a professor of moral philosophy at South Carolina College.

**793.** Miles, James Warley. *The Discourse on the Occasion of the Funeral of the Hon. John C. Calhoun, Delivered under the Appointment of the Joint Committee of the City Council and Citizens of Charleston. At St. Philip's Church, April 26th, 1850.* Charleston: J. Russell, 1850. Miles was a theologian.

**794.** [Minor, Lucian?]. "A Few Thoughts on the Death of John C. Calhoun." *Southern Literary Messenger* 16 (May 1850): 376–379. Includes recollections of conversations with Calhoun.

**795.** M[oore], S.D. "John Caldwell Calhoun." *Southern Quarterly Review* 18 (November 1850): 486–509. An Alabama eulogy.

**796.** *Obituary Addresses Delivered on the Occasion of the Death of John C. Calhoun, a Senator of South Carolina, in the Senate of the United States, April 1, 1850. With the Funeral Sermon of the Rev. C.M. Butler, Presented in the Senate, April 2, 1850.* Washington: John T. Towers, 1850. Tributes by Daniel Webster, Henry Clay, and others.

**797.** Rogers, William W. "The South Mourns a Leader: The Death of John C. Calhoun." *Alabama Historical Quarterly* 36 (Summer 1974): 167–171. Review of public reaction.

**798.** Smith, Whitefoord. *The Rectitude of Divine Administration: A Discourse Suggested by the Death of Hon. J.C. Calhoun. Delivered in the Methodist Church of Columbia, S.C., on Sunday, April 7th, 1850.* Columbia: Johnston & Davis, 1850. By a leader of the Southern Methodists.

**799.** South Carolina General Assembly. *The Death and Funeral Ceremonies of John Caldwell Calhoun, Containing the Speeches, Reports, and Other Documents Connected Therewith; the Oration of the Hon. R.B. Rhett, before the Legislature, &c.* Columbia, S.C.: A.S. Johnston, 1850.

**800.** Thomas, John Peyre, ed. *The Carolina Tribute to Calhoun.* Columbia. S.C.: Richard L. Bryan, 1857. Memorial tributes and reminiscences by South Carolina contemporaries. Contains most of the best sermons and eulogies of the time, many of which were separately published as well.

**801.** Thornwell, James H. *Thoughts Suited to the Present Crisis: A Sermon, on Occasion of the Death of Hon. John C. Calhoun, Preached in the Chapel of South Carolina College, April 21, 1850.* Columbia, S.C.: published by the students, 1850. A noted Presbyterian theologian and president of South Carolina College.

**802.** Yancey, William Lowndes. *Address on the Life and Character of John C. Calhoun.* Montgomery, Ala.: Advertiser & Gazette, 1850. A leading Southern orator.

# VI.
# John C. Calhoun's Associates

### A. NATIONAL FIGURES

ADAMS, JOHN QUINCY

**803.** Bemis, Samuel Flagg. *John Quincy Adams and the Foundations of American Foreign Policy.* New York: Alfred A. Knopf, 1949.

**804.** ———. *John Quincy Adams and the Union.* New York: Alfred A. Knopf, 1956.

**805.** Richards, Leonard L. *The Life and Times of Congressman John Quincy Adams.* New York: Oxford University Press, 1986. Adams during the later years when Calhoun called him "a mischievous, bad old man."
See also # 608.

BENTON, THOMAS H.

**806.** Chambers, William Nisbet. *Old Bullion Benton: Senator from the New West.* Boston: Little, Brown & Co., 1956.
See also # 966.

BIDDLE, NICHOLAS

**807.** Govan, Thomas Payne. *Nicholas Biddle: Nationalist and Banker.* Chicago: University of Chicago Press, 1959.

BLAIR, FRANCIS P.

**808.** Smith, William E. *The Francis Preston Blair Family in Politics.*

2 vols. New York: Macmillan, 1933. The Blairs, owners of the Washington *Globe,* were key figures in orchestrating opposition to Calhoun within the Democratic party.

BUCHANAN, JAMES

**809.** Curtis, George T. *Life of James Buchanan.* 2 vols. New York: Harper, 1883.

CASS, LEWIS

**810.** Smith, W. L. G. *Life and Times of Lewis Cass.* New York: Derby and Jackson, 1856. Cass was a major Democratic politician of the Northwest whose career often intersected Calhoun's as collaborator or rival.

**811.** Woodward, Frank B. *Lewis Cass: The Last Jeffersonian.* New Brunswick, N.J.: Rutgers University Press, 1950. Cass's career paralleled Calhoun's with occasional interchange, especially in Calhoun's War Department period.

CLAY, HENRY

**812.** Eaton, Clement. *Henry Clay and the Art of American Politics.* Boston: Little, Brown & Co., 1957.

See also #393.

CRAWFORD, WILLIAM H.

**813.** Mooney, Chase C. *William H. Crawford, 1772–1834.* Lexington, Ky.: University Press of Kentucky, 1974. Biography of Calhoun's rival in the Monroe cabinet and election of 1824.

See also # 149, 587.

DALLAS, GEORGE M.

**814.** Belohlavek, John M. *George Mifflin Dallas: Jacksonian Patrician.* University Park, Pa., and London: Pennsylvania State University Press, 1977. This senator from Pa., diplomat, and vice president was on close terms with Calhoun.

INGERSOLL, CHARLES J.

See #156.

## JACKSON, ANDREW

**815.** Bassett, John Spencer. *The Life of Andrew Jackson*, 2 vols. in 1. New York: Macmillan, 1916. Still a readable and balanced account of Jackson's life.

See also # 390, 558, 677.

## JOHNSON, RICHARD M.

**816.** Meyer, Leland M. *The Life and Times of Colonel Richard M. Johnson of Kentucky.* New York: Columbia University Press, 1932. The life of this frontiersman and vice president involved much contact with Calhoun.

## McLANE, LOUIS

**817.** Munroe, John A. *Louis McLane: Federalist and Jacksonian.* New Brunswick, N.J.: Rutgers University Press, 1973. This Delaware political leader, secretary of state and treasury, and diplomat, was on good terms with Calhoun.

## McLEAN, JOHN

**818.** Weisenburger, Francis P. *The Life of John McLean, a Politician on the United States Supreme Court.* Columbus, Ohio: Ohio State University Press, 1937. McLean's career paralleled Calhoun's, and like Calhoun he exercised influence somewhat independently of political parties.

## MADISON, JAMES

**819.** Ketcham, Ralph. *James Madison: A Biography.* New York: Macmillan, 1971.

See also # 520, 637.

## MONROE, JAMES

See # 537.

## POLK, JAMES K.

**820.** Sellers, Charles G. *James K. Polk.* 2 vols. Princeton, N.J.: Princeton University Press, 1957–1966.

See also # 762.

RITCHIE, THOMAS

See # 513.

SCOTT, WINFIELD

**821.** Elliott, Charles Winslow. *Winfield Scott: The Soldier and the Man.* New York: Macmillan, 1937.

See also # 562.

SMITH, SAMUEL

**822.** Pancake, John S. *Samuel Smith and the Politics of Business, 1752–1839.* Tuscaloosa, Ala.: University of Alabama Press, 1972. This Maryland political leader was an important figure in the late Jeffersonian and early Jacksonian eras.

TANEY, ROGER B.

**823.** Swisher, Carl Brent. *Roger B. Taney.* New York: Macmillan, 1935.

**824.** Tyler, Samuel. *Memoir of Roger Brooke Taney, LL.D.* Baltimore: John Murray & Co., 1876. Occasional sympathetic references to Calhoun by the Jacksonian secretary of the treasury and chief justice.

TAZEWELL, LITTLETON W.

**825.** Peterson, Norma Lois. *Littleton Waller Tazewell.* Charlottesville, Va.: University Press of Virginia, 1983. Though almost forgotten, Tazewell was a very important Virginia politician of the Jacksonian period and often a close associate of Calhoun.

TYLER, JOHN

See # 166, 713, 714, 715, 716.

VAN BUREN, MARTIN

**826.** Alexander, Holmes M. *The American Talleyrand: The Career and Contemporaries of Martin Van Buren, the Eighth President.* New York: Harper, 1935. Van Buren somewhat as seen by Calhoun's friends.

# John C. Calhoun's Associates

**827.** Cole, Donald B. *Martin Van Buren and the American Political System*. Princeton, N.J.: Princeton University Press, 1984. Probably the best biography.

**828.** Niven, John. *Martin Van Buren: The Romantic Age of American Politics*. New York: Oxford University Press, 1983. A biography perhaps most useful for its great political detail.

**829.** Van Buren, Martin. "The Autobiography of Martin Van Buren." Edited by John C. Fitzpatrick. In *American Historical Association Annual Report* for 1918, vol. 2. Washington: U.S. Government Printing Office, 1920. The sometimes candid, sometimes cagey memoirs of the great architect of issueless party politics.
See also # 620, 682.

WALKER, ROBERT J.

**830.** Shenton, James P. *Robert John Walker: A Politician from Jackson to Lincoln*. New York and London: Columbia University Press, 1961. Biography of Walker, senator from Mississippi, secretary of the treasury under Polk, and sometime Calhoun ally.

WEBSTER, DANIEL

**831.** Bartlett, Irving H. *Daniel Webster*. New York: W. W. Norton, 1978.

**832.** ———. "The Double Character of Daniel Webster." *New England Journal of Public Policy* 3 (Winter/Spring 1987): 39–50.
See also # 393.

WHEATON, HENRY

**833.** Baker, Elizabeth F. *Henry Wheaton, 1785–1848*. Philadelphia: University of Pennsylvania Press, 1937; reprint, New York: De Capo Press, 1971. Henry Wheaton of New York was a leading American scholar and diplomat of the day, with whom Calhoun had a long and cordial relationship.

WISE, HENRY A.

**834.** Simpson, Craig M. *A Good Southerner: The Life of Henry A. Wise*. Chapel Hill, N.C.: University of North Carolina Press, 1985.

Wise was a key advisor to President Tyler and U. S. Minister to Brazil while Calhoun was secretary of state.

See also # 717.

WRIGHT, SILAS

**835.** Garraty, John A. *Silas Wright.* New York: Columbia University Press, 1949. Governor and senator from New York and Van Buren's chief lieutenant.

## B. SOUTH CAROLINIANS

CHEVES, LANGDON

**836.** Huff, Archie Vernon. *Langdon Cheves of South Carolina.* Columbia, S.C.: University of South Carolina Press, 1977. Speaker of the U.S. House of Representatives and president of the Bank of the United States, Cheves was a longtime Calhoun ally.

CLEMSON, THOMAS G.

See # 907, 910.

COOPER, THOMAS

**837.** Malone, Dumas. *The Public Life of Thomas Cooper, 1783–1839.* Columbia, S.C.: University of South Carolina Press, 1961. The career and thought of the fiery Nullifier and president of South Carolina College.

DAVIS, WARREN R.

**838.** Perry, Benjamin F. "Warren R. Davis." In *The Writings of Benjamin F. Perry.* Edited by Stephen Meats and Edwin T. Arnold. 3 vols. Spartanburg, S.C.: Reprint Co., 1980, 2:160–164. Sketch of an able Calhoun protegé and South Carolina congressman who died young.

ELMORE, FRANKLIN H.

**839.** Hamilton, J. G. de Roulhac. "Franklin Harper Elmore." In *Dictionary of American Biography.* Edited by Allen Johnson and Dumas Malone. 22 vols. New York: Charles Scribner's Sons, 1928–1944,

6:118–119. Elmore was Calhoun's most important lieutenant in South Carolina.

**840.** Lesesne, J. Mauldin. *The Bank of the State of South Carolina: A General and Political History*. Columbia, S.C.: University of South Carolina Press, 1970. An important and controversial institution headed by Calhoun's ally Franklin H. Elmore.

**841.** Perry, Benjamin F. "Franklin H. Elmore." In *The Writings of Benjamin F. Perry*. Edited by Stephen Meats and Edwin T. Arnold. 3 vols. Spartanburg, S.C.: Reprint Co., 1980, 2:220–224. First-hand recollections of one of Calhoun's chief lieutenants by an enemy.

GADSDEN, JAMES

**842.** Garber, Paul N. *The Gadsden Treaty*. Philadelphia: University of Pennsylvania Press, 1923. James Gadsden, soldier, railroad president, and diplomat, was a longtime close associate of Calhoun.

GREGG, WILLIAM

**843.** Mitchell, Broadus. *William Gregg: Factory Maker of the Old South*. Chapel Hill, N.C.: University of North Carolina Press, 1928. The leading industrialist in South Carolina in Calhoun's time.

HAMILTON, JAMES, JR.

**844.** Glenn, Virginia Louise. "James Hamilton, Jr., of South Carolina: A Biography." Ph.D. dissertation, University of North Carolina, 1964. Hamilton, the fiery Nullification governor of South Carolina, later a diplomat of the Texas Republic, was a longtime Calhoun ally.

**845.** Perry, Benjamin F. "James Hamilton, Jr." In *The Writings of Benjamin F. Perry*. Edited by Stephen Meats and Edwin T. Arnold. 3 vols. Spartanburg, S.C.: Reprint Co., 1980, 2:320–324. A key figure in the South Carolina Nullification movement.

See also # 666.

HAMMOND, JAMES H.

**846.** Faust, Drew Gilpin. *James Henry Hammond and the Old South: A Design for Mastery*. Baton Rouge, La.: Louisiana State University Press, 1982. Psycho-biography, light on politics and ideas.

**847.** Hammond, James Henry. *Selections from the Letters and Speeches of the Hon. James H. Hammond, of South Carolina.* Edited by Clyde N. Wilson. Spartanburg, S.C.: Reprint Co., 1978 (originally published 1866). The public statements of one of the most intellectually able of Calhoun's South Carolina lieutenants.

**848.** Merritt, Elizabeth. *James Henry Hammond 1807–1864.* Baltimore: Johns Hopkins Press, 1923.

**849.** Tucker, Robert C. "James Henry Hammond: South Carolinian." Ph.D. dissertation, University of North Carolina, 1958.

HAYNE, ROBERT Y.

**850.** Jervey, Theodore D. *Robert Y. Hayne and His Times.* New York: Macmillan, 1909. Biography of a Calhoun ally and surrogate.

LEGARÉ, HUGH S.

**851.** O'Brien, Michael. *A Character of Hugh Legaré.* Knoxville, Tenn.: University of Tennessee Press, 1985. A Charleston intellectual and sometime critic of Calhoun.

**852.** Rhea, Linda. *Hugh Swinton Legaré: A Charleston Intellectual.* Chapel Hill, N.C.: University of North Carolina Press, 1934.

LIEBER, FRANCIS

**853.** Freidel, Frank. *Francis Lieber: Nineteenth Century Liberal.* Baton Rouge, La.: Louisiana State University Press, 1947. The German-born professor of political science at South Carolina College who later moved North.

LOWNDES, WILLIAM

See # 522, 524.

McDUFFIE, GEORGE

**854.** Fletcher, Ralph Henry. "George McDuffie: Orator and Politician." M.A. thesis, University of South Carolina, 1986. Study of a close associate of Calhoun, governor, senator, and fiery orator.

**855.** Green, Edwin L. *George McDuffie*. Columbia, S.C.: The State Co., 1936.

ORR, JAMES L.

**856.** Leemhuis, Roger P. *James L. Orr and the Sectional Conflict*. Washington: University Press of America, 1979. Orr perhaps best represented Calhoun's viewpoint in national politics after Calhoun's death.

PERRY, BENJAMIN F.

**857.** Kibler, Lillian Adele. *Benjamin F. Perry: South Carolina Unionist*. Durham, N.C.: Duke University Press, 1946. Essential to the understanding of the nature of South Carolina "Unionism."

PETIGRU, JAMES L.

**858.** Carson, James Petigru. *Life, Letters and Speeches of James Louis Petigru, the Union Man of South Carolina*. Washington: W. H. Lowdermilk & Co., 1920. Career and viewpoint of Calhoun's chief "Unionist" critic within South Carolina.

**859.** Grayson, William John. *James Louis Petigru, A Biographical Sketch*. New York: Harper & Brothers, 1866.

**860.** *Memorial of the Late James L. Petigru: Proceedings of the Bar of Charleston, S.C., March 25, 1863*. Charleston, S.C.: Walker, Evans & Cogswell, 1880.

**861.** Wilson, Clyde N. *Carolina Cavalier: The Life and Mind of James Johnston Pettigrew*. Athens, Ga.: University of Georgia Press, 1990. Critical opinions of Calhoun's policies and influence by James L. Petigru and his North Carolina and South Carolina friends and relatives.

PICKENS, FRANCIS W.

**862.** Edmunds, John B. *Francis W. Pickens and the Politics of Destruction*. Chapel Hill, N.C.: University of North Carolina Press, 1986. Critical biography of a South Carolina political leader who was a kinsman and follower of Calhoun.

POINSETT, JOEL R.

**863.** Rippy, J. Fred. *Joel R. Poinsett: Versatile American.* Durham, N.C.: Duke University Press, 1946. Diplomat and secretary of war, Poinsett was a "Unionist" national Democrat.

PRESTON, WILLIAM C.

**864.** Preston, William C. *The Reminiscences of William C. Preston.* Edited by Minnie Clare Yarborough. Chapel Hill, N.C.: University of North Carolina Press, 1933. Senator from South Carolina and president of South Carolina College, Preston went from "Nullifier" to Calhoun's chief Whig critic in the state.

RHETT, ROBERT BARNWELL

**865.** White, Laura A. *Robert Barnwell Rhett: Father of Secession.* New York: Appleton-Century-Crofts, 1931. Biography of Calhoun's rebellious disciple; essential for the understanding of South Carolina "fire-eaters."

SIMMS, WILLIAM GILMORE

**866.** Butterworth, Keen. "William Gilmore Simms." In *Antebellum Writers in New York and the South,* ed. by Joel Myerson (Vol. 3 of *Dictionary of Literary Biography*), pp. 306–319. Detroit: Gale Research Co., 1979. Best biography of the leading man of letters of South Carolina in Calhoun's time.

**867.** Guilds, John Caldwell, ed. *"Long Years of Neglect": The Work and Reputation of William Gilmore Simms.* Fayetteville, Ark., and London: University of Arkansas Press, 1989. A dozen scholars reassess the leading South Carolina literary figure contemporary to Calhoun.
See also # 165.

THOMPSON, WADDY

**868.** Thompson, Henry T. *General Waddy Thompson.* Columbia, S.C.: no publisher, 1929. Representative from South Carolina and diplomat, Thompson went from "Nullifier" to Whig critic of Calhoun.

## THORNWELL, JAMES H.

**869.** Farmer, James O. *The Metaphysical Confederacy: James Henley Thornwell and the Synthesis of Southern Values*. Macon, Ga.: Mercer University Press, 1986. Study of the president of South Carolina College and Presbyterian theologian who is often called "the Calhoun of the church."

**870.** Genovese, Eugene D. "James Thornwell and Southern Religion." *Southern Partisan* 7 (Summer 1987): 16–21.

**871.** Thornwell, James Henley. *The Collected Writings of James Henley Thornwell*. 4 vols. Edited by Benjamin M. Palmer. Richmond: Presbyterian Publications Committee, 1871–1873.

## WILLIAMS, DAVID R.

**872.** Cook, Harvey T. *The Life and Legacy of David Rogerson Williams*. New York: Country Life Press, 1916. Williams was a "War Hawk" colleague of Calhoun, governor of South Carolina, and a pioneer industrialist.

## C. LIEUTENANTS AND ALLIES IN OTHER STATES

## BROWNSON, ORESTES A.

**873.** Brownson, Orestes A. *The Works of Orestes A. Brownson*. 20 vols. Edited by Henry F. Brownson. Detroit: T. Nourse, 1882–1887.

**874.** Schlesinger, Arthur M., Jr. *Orestes A. Brownson: A Pilgrim's Progress*. New York: Octagon Books, 1963 (originally published 1939). See also # 31, 145.

## CRALLÉ, RICHARD K.

**875.** Moore, Frederick W. "Richard Kenner Crallé." In *Publications of the Southern History Association* 7 (May 1903): 163–164. Only biographical treatment of the Virginia editor who was Calhoun's chief clerk in the State Department and the editor of Calhoun's *Works*.

## GREEN, BEN E.

**876.** Green, Fletcher M. "Benjamin Edwards Green." In *Dictionary of American Biography*. Edited by Allen Johnson and Dumas Malone.

22 vols. New York: Charles Scribner's Sons, 1928–1944, 7:538–539. Brief biography of Duff Green's son—diplomat, economist, and Calhoun apologist.

GREEN, DUFF

**877.** Green, Duff. *Facts and Suggestions, Biographical, Historical, Financial, and Political, Addressed to the People of the United States.* New York: Richardson, 1866. The post-Civil War reflections of one of Calhoun's closest associates.

**878.** Green, Fletcher M. "Duff Green." In *Dictionary of American Biography.* Edited by Allen Johnson and Dumas Malone. 22 vols. New York: Charles Scribner's Sons, 1928–1944, 7:540–542. Succinct biography of an important Calhoun lieutenant.

**879.** ———. "Duff Green." In *Encyclopedia Britannica.* 24 vols. Chicago: Encyclopedia Britannica, Inc., 1963, 10:851.

**880.** ———. "Duff Green: Industrial Promoter." *Journal of Southern History* 2 (February 1936): 29–42. The remarkable entrepreneurial career of the "Calhoun of the Economy."

**881.** ———. "Duff Green: Militant Journalist of the Old School." *American Historical Review* 52 (January 1947): 247–264. Green's career as newspaper publisher and editor in behalf of Calhoun and Southern economic development.

**882.** Wilson, Clyde N. "Duff Green: Some Notes Toward a Biography." Unpublished paper presented at Columbia, S.C., October 10, 1988.

HUNTER, ROBERT M. T.

**883.** Fisher, John E. "Statesman of the Lost Cause: R. M. T. Hunter and the Sectional Controversy, 1847–1887." Ph.D. dissertation, University of Virginia, 1968. The later career of Calhoun's chief Virginia lieutenant.

**884.** Simms, Henry H. *Life of Robert M. T. Hunter.* Richmond, Va.: William Byrd Press, 1935.

See also # 155, 675.

## INGHAM, SAMUEL D.

**885.** Ingham, William D. "Samuel D. Ingham, Secretary of the U.S. Treasury." *Bucks County Historical Society Papers* 4 (1917): 19–30. Representative from Pennsylvania and secretary of the treasury, Ingham was a longtime Calhoun friend.

## LEWIS, DIXON H.

**886.** Martin, John M. "John C. Calhoun and Dixon H. Lewis: Partners in Politics." Unpublished paper presented to Ohio Valley History Conference, October 1985.

**887.** Moore, Frederick W. "Dixon Hall Lewis." In *Publications of the Southern History Association* 7 (May 1903): 161–162. The Alabama political leader who was Calhoun's congressional manager.

## LONGSTREET, A. B.

**888.** Scafidel, James R. "The Letters of Augustus Baldwin Longstreet." Ph.D. dissertation, University of South Carolina, 1976. The public and private writings of a Southern author, college president, and clergyman, who was a longtime friend and defender of Calhoun. See also # 430.

## MAXCY, VIRGIL

**889.** Kelly, J. R. "Tulip Hill, Its History and Its People." *Maryland Historical Magazine* 60 (December 1965): 349–403. Biographical material on Virgil Maxcy, Calhoun's most intimate friend, through the history of his Maryland plantation.

**890.** Thomson, Irving L. "Virgil Maxcy." In *Dictionary of American Biography*. Edited by Allen Johnson and Dumas Malone. 22 vols. New York: Charles Scribner's Sons, 1928–1944, 12:434–435.

## SCOVILLE, JOSEPH A.

**891.** [Scoville, Joseph A.] *Vigor. A Novel. "By Walter Barrett, Clerk."* New York: Carleton, Publisher, 1864. Lightly fictionalized autobiography of Calhoun's one-time secretary, a New York writer and merchant.

SEDDON, JAMES A.

**892.** Curry, Roy W. "James A. Seddon, a Southern Prototype." *Virginia Magazine of History and Biography* 63 (April 1955): 123–150. One of Calhoun's Virginia followers.

UPSHUR, ABEL P.

**893.** Hall, Claude H. *Abel Parker Upshur, Conservative Virginian, 1790–1844.* Madison, Wis.: State Historical Society of Wisconsin, 1964. Secretary of State Upshur was a close Calhoun collaborator. See also # 718.

# VII.
# Personal Life of John C. Calhoun

### A. GENERAL

**894.** Bates, Mary. *The Private Life of John C. Calhoun.* Charleston, S.C.: Walker and Richards, 1852. Recollections by a Northern-born tutor who lived for several years with Calhoun's family.

**895.** Bradford, Gamaliel. "John Caldwell Calhoun." In *As God Made Them. Portraits of Some Nineteenth-Century Americans.* Boston and New York: Houghton Mifflin Co., 1929. Psychological portrait (pp. 84–127).

**896.** Coit, Margaret L., ed. *John C. Calhoun.* Englewood Cliffs, N.J.: Prentice-Hall, 1970. A collection of observations of Calhoun.

**897.** Cook, Harriet Hefner. *John C. Calhoun—the Man.* Columbia, S.C.: privately printed, 1965. A description of the "human side and home life," well illustrated.

**898.** *John C. Calhoun, in His Personal, Moral and Intellectual Traits of Character.* New York: *Daily Morning Post,* [1843]. Contemporary human interest treatment.

**899.** Miller, Walter. "Calhoun as a Lawyer and Statesman." *The Green Bag* 11 (May–September 1899): 197–203, 269–277, 326–337, 419–426. Interesting anecdotal material.

**900.** Scoville, Joseph A. "Mr. Calhoun's Dying Hours." *Living Age,* November 11, 1854, pp. 265–266. A discussion of Calhoun's last hours and religious views by his one-time secretary.

**901.** Wilson, Clyde N. Introduction to Wilson, ed., *The Papers of John C. Calhoun,* vol. 14, *1837–1839,* pp. xi–xxxiii. Columbia, S.C.: University of South Carolina Press, 1981. Analyzes Calhoun's personality, home life, and political strategy during the later 1830s.

## B. WIFE, CHILDREN, OTHER RELATIVES, AND DESCENDANTS

**902.** Chappell, Buford S. *The Chappell Family in Early South Carolina.* Columbia, S.C.: R. L. Bryan Co., 1972. In-laws of John C. Calhoun.

**903.** Day, Kate Pickens. *Cousin Monroe's History of the Pickens Family.* Greenville, S.C.: Hiott Press, 1951. A family closely related to Calhoun by marriage and association.

**904.** DuBose, John W. *The Life and Times of William Lowndes Yancey.* Birmingham, Ala.: Roberts & Son, 1892. Material on Calhoun's agricultural and family visiting trips to Alabama.

**905.** Fox-Genovese, Elizabeth. *Within the Plantation Household: Black and White Women of the Old South.* Chapel Hill, N.C., and London: University of North Carolina Press, 1988. Occasional comments on Mrs. Calhoun.

**906.** History Group, Inc. *Historical Investigations of the Richard B. Russell Multiple Resource Area.* Atlanta: U.S. National Park Service, 1981. Extensive study of the huge and diverse plantation, Millwood, operated by Calhoun's brother-in-law, James Edward Colhoun, in Abbeville District (pp. 177–193).

**907.** Holmes, Alester G., and George R. Sherrill. *Thomas Green Clemson: His Life and Work.* Richmond, Va.: Garrett and Massie, 1937. Only full-length biography of Calhoun's son-in-law, concentrating on his public career as scientist and diplomat.

**908.** "John C. Calhoun's Home Life." In Spartanburg, S.C., *Carolina Spartan,* August 16, 1866. Unsigned local recollections of the Calhoun family on the occasion of Mrs. Calhoun's obituary.

**909.** "John C. Calhoun's Home Life." Anderson, S.C., *Daily Mail,* October 23, 1926. Unsigned recollections dating from 1849.

**910.** Lander, Ernest M. *The Calhoun Family and Thomas Green Clemson: The Decline of a Southern Patriarchy.* Columbia, S.C.: University of South Carolina Press, 1983. Unsympathetic history of Calhoun's children and grandchildren.

**911.** ———. "Mrs. John C. Calhoun and the Coming of the Civil War." *Civil War History* 22 (December 1976): 308–317. Account of Calhoun's widow.

**912.** ———. "Mrs. John C. Calhoun and the Death of Patrick." *South Carolina Review* 9 (November 1976): 52–59. Account of Calhoun's widow and her second son.

**913.** McGee, Charles M., and Ernest M. Lander, eds. *A Rebel Came Home: the Diary of Floride Clemson.* Columbia, S.C.: University of South Carolina Press, 1961; revised 1989. Civil War experiences of Calhoun's granddaughter.

**914.** Moore, W. Allan, Jr. "The Bonneau Family." *Transactions of the Huguenot Society of South Carolina* 52 (1947): 38–39. Calhoun's mother-in-law's family.

**915.** Moragné, Mary E. *The Neglected Thread: A Journal from the Calhoun Community, 1836–1846.* Edited by Delle Mullen Craven. Columbia, S.C.: University of South Carolina Press, 1951. Firsthand account of Calhoun's native Abbeville neighborhood where he had many relatives and often visited.

**916.** Phifer, Robert S. *Notes on the Pickens, Calhoun, Simkins, Wilkinson, Morton, Middleton Families.* Typescript, 1945. Material compiled from ms. records (copy in the South Caroliniana Library, University of South Carolina).

**917.** Rembert, Sarah H. "Barhamville: A Columbia Antebellum Girls' School." *South Carolina History Illustrated* 1 (February 1970): 44–48. The institution attended by Anna Maria Calhoun, daughter of John C. Calhoun.

**918.** "Simkins Family Graveyard is Cleared and Epitaphs Again Become Readable; Reveal Much Interesting Information." Columbia, S.C., *State*, January 6, 1935. The family of Eldred Simkins who was Calhoun's law partner and related to the Calhouns by marriage several times over.

**919.** Symonds, G. W. "When He Went A-Wooing." *Ladies' Home Journal* 18 (May 1901):6. Popular account of Calhoun's courtship.

**920.** Wick, Mildred Calhoun. *Living with Love.* Newport, Del.: Serendipity Press, 1986. Well-illustrated family history of Calhoun's descendants.

## C. FORT HILL AND PENDLETON

**921.** *A Future for the Past.* Pendleton, S.C.: Foundation for Historic Preservation in the Pendleton Area, 1961. Descriptions and histories of Fort Hill and neighboring homes.

**922.** Godwin, Parke. "Calhoun." In *Homes of American Statesmen: with Anecdotical, Personal, and Descriptive Sketches, by Various Writers.* New York: Alfred W. Upham, 1860. Contemporary description of Fort Hill.

**923.** "The Home Where Clemson Began." *Southern Living* 19 (August 1984): 28–29. Description of Fort Hill.

**924.** "Hon. John C. Calhoun's Farm." *Carolina Planter* 1 (April 1845): 219–221. An agricultural society report on the superior management of Calhoun's farming operations at Fort Hill.

**925.** Howe, Henry. *Our Whole Country: of the Past and Present of the United States, Historical and Descriptive.* 2 vols. New York: Tuttle & McCauley, 1863. Contemporary description and drawings of Fort Hill (1:724–727).

**926.** Ingersoll, Ernest. "The Calhoun Summer Home." *Scribner's Monthly* 21 (April 1881): 892–895. Interesting late 19th century description of "Fort Hill," with drawings.

**927.** McFall, Pearl Smith. *So Lives the Dream; History and Story of the Old Pendleton District, South Carolina, and the Establishment of Clemson College.* New York: Comet Press, 1953. Local history of Calhoun's neighborhood.

**928.** [Newmann, C. L., and J. C. Stribling.] *The Pendleton Farmers' Society.* Atlanta: Foote and Davies Co., 1908. History of a local agricultural society of which Calhoun was a founding member and one-time president.

**929.** [Scoville, Joseph A.] "A Visit to Fort Hill." New York *Herald*, July 26, 1849.

**930.** Simpson, Richard W. *History of Old Pendleton District.* Anderson, S.C.: Oula Printing Co., 1913. History of the Calhoun neighborhood by a family friend.

**931.** Sloan, Dave M. *Fogy Days, and Now; or, The World Has Changed.* Atlanta: Foote & Davies, 1891. Pendleton recollections.

**932.** Topographic Map of John C. Calhoun's Plantation. Clemson University College of Architecture, *ca.* 1971. Reconstruction of now-vanished topography, agricultural operations, and buildings.

**933.** Wilson, Clyde N. Introduction to Wilson, ed., *The Papers of John C. Calhoun,* vol. 16, *1841–1843,* pp. ix–xxxii. Columbia, S.C.: University of South Carolina Press, 1984. Calhoun's agricultural operations.

## D. THE CALHOUN GOLD MINE

**934.** Birdsall, C. M. *The United States Branch Mint at Dahlonega, Ga.: Its History and Coinage.* Easley, S.C.: Southern Historical Press, 1984. Material on Calhoun's gold mine near Dahlonega.

**935.** Boatright, Sherry L. "The John C. Calhoun Gold Mine: An Introductory Report on its Historical Significance." [Atlanta:] Georgia Department of Historical Resources, Historic Preservation Section, 1974. Study of the gold mine owned by Calhoun for many years near Dahlonega, Ga.

**936.** Bryan, T. Conn. "The Gold Rush in Georgia." *Georgia Review* 9 (Winter 1955): 1–7.

**937.** Head, Sylvia G., and Elizabeth W. Ethridge. *The Neighborhood Mint. Dahlonega in the Age of Jackson.* Macon, Ga.: Mercer University Press, 1986. Portrait of the town and mint with which Calhoun was closely involved.

**938.** Jones, S. P. *Second Report on the Gold Deposits of Georgia* (Geological Survey of Georgia Bulletin No. 19). Atlanta: Charles P. Byrd, 1909. Material on the gold mine owned by Calhoun near Dahlonega, Ga.

**939.** Yeates, W. S., and others. *A Preliminary Report on a Part of the Gold Deposits of Georgia* (Geological Survey of Georgia Bulletin

No. 4-A). Atlanta: 1896. Material on the gold mine owned by Calhoun near Dahlonega.

940. Young, Otis E., Jr. "The Southern Gold Rush, 1828–1836." *Journal of Southern History* 48 (August 1982): 373–392.

### E. MISCELLANY

941. Alley, Felix E. "Abraham Lincoln was a Native of the Carolina Mountains." In Alley's *Random Thoughts and the Musings of a Mountaineer.* Salisbury, N.C.: Rowan Printing Co., 1941. The most elaborate published polemic for the curious perennial legend that Calhoun was the natural father of Lincoln.

942. Barton, William E. *The Paternity of Abraham Lincoln.* New York: George H. Doran Co., 1920. Two chapters are devoted to investigation of the myth of Calhoun's paternity to Lincoln, with the conclusion that the claim though interesting has no merit.

943. "Exhumation of the Body of John C. Calhoun, 1863." *South Carolina Historical Magazine* 57 (January 1956): 57–58. Account of the hiding of Calhoun's body during the Civil War to prevent desecration by federal troops.

944. Federal Writers' Project. *Washington: City and Capital.* Washington: U.S. Government Printing Office, 1937. History of the Georgetown estate "Dumbarton Oaks," once owned by Calhoun (pp. 743–744).

945. Jaccaud, Robert D. "The Calhoun Collection of Pamphlets and the Presidential Election of 1824." *Dartmouth College Library Bulletin* 13 (November 1972): 48–58. Description of a portion of Calhoun's dispersed library.

946. "The Library of John C. Calhoun." *De Bow's Review,* new series 6 (July 1869): 594. Report and discussion of the dispersal of Calhoun's library on the death of his eldest son.

947. Mouat, Linda. "Museum Treasure Hunt: Dumbarton Oaks, Washington, D.C." *Christian Science Monitor,* August 24, 1971, p. 6. Calhoun's Georgetown home in modern reincarnation.

**948.** Ringgold, Mary Spencer. "John C. Calhoun: Post Mortem." *Emory University Quarterly* 6 (March 1955): 98–102. The Civil War disinterment and reburial of Calhoun's remains.

### F. SELECTED FIRST-HAND ENCOUNTERS

**949.** Atwater, Caleb. *Mysteries of Washington City, during Several Months of the Session of the 28th Congress. By a Citizen of Ohio.* Washington: G. A. Sage, 1844. Calhoun interviews with a visiting writer (pp. 169–176).

**950.** Curry, J. L. M. *Civil History of the Government of the Confederate States, with Some Personal Reminiscences.* Richmond, Va.: B. F. Johnson, 1901. Vivid description of Calhoun by a young man who was later an Alabama congressman and educator (pp. 19–21).

**951.** Davis, Jefferson. "Life and Character of the Hon. John Caldwell Calhoun." *North American Review* 145 (September 1887): 246–260. Personal recollections by the president of the Confederate States.

**952.** Davis, Varina Howell. *Jefferson Davis: A Memoir.* 2 vols. New York: Belford Co., 1890. Youthful recollections of the wife of Jefferson Davis (1:209–214).

**953.** Dyer, Oliver. *Great Senators of the United States Forty Years Ago.* New York: R. Bonner's Sons, 1889. An abolitionist charmed by Calhoun.

**954.** Featherstonhaugh, George W. *A Canoe Voyage up the Minnay Sotor.* 2 vols. St. Paul, Minn.: Minnesota Historical Society, 1970 (first published 1847). A visiting English scientist who shared Calhoun's interest in Appalachian exploration and mining (2:247–271).

**955.** Grund, Francis J. *Aristocracy in America,* 2 vols. London: Richard Bentley, 1839. A much-travelled German observer (2:297–298).

**956.** Healy, George P. A. *Reminiscences of a Portrait Painter.* Chicago: A C. McClurg, 1894. Chatty memoirs of an artist who painted Calhoun several times.

**957.** Martineau, Harriet. *Retrospect of Western Travel.* 2 vols. London: Saunders & Otley, 1838. An English woman writer (1:147–149).

**958.** Maury, Sarah Mytton. *The Statesmen of America in 1846.* Philadelphia: Carey and Hart, 1847. Sympathetic portrait by an English writer (pp. 168–184).

**959.** Pollard, Edward A. "Personal Recollections of John C. Calhoun." New York *Citizen,* May 9, 1869. By a leading Southern journalist.

**960.** Raumer, Frederick von. *America and the American People.* Translated from the German by William W. Turner. New York: J. & H. G. Langley, 1846. An admiring German historian.

**961.** Smith, Margaret Bayard. *The First Forty Years of Washington Society, Portrayed by the Family Letters of Mrs. Samuel Harrison Smith (Margaret Bayard). . . .* Edited by Gaillard Hunt. New York: Charles Scribner's Sons, 1906. A fixture of Washington society well acquainted with the Calhouns.

**962.** Wentworth, John W. *Congressional Reminiscences. Adams, Benton, Calhoun, Clay, and Webster.* Chicago: Fergus Printing Co., 1882. Memoirs of an Illinois congressman of abolitionist leanings (pp. 20–25).

**963.** Wikoff, Henry. *Reminiscences of an Idler.* New York: Fords, Howard, & Hulbert, 1880. Anecdotes and observations by a Philadelphia playboy who once financed a Calhoun newspaper in New York City.

# VIII.
# Historical Evaluation of John C. Calhoun

### A. PUBLIC CAREER

**964.** Ashley, James M. *Reminiscences of the Great Rebellion: Calhoun, Seward and Lincoln.* Toledo, Ohio: no publisher, 1890. "Bloody shirt" lecture by a Radical Republican.

**965.** Basso, Hamilton. "John C. Calhoun of Fort Hill: The American as Aristocrat." In Basso, *Mainstream.* New York: Reynal and Hitchcock, 1943, pp. 44–63. Shallow portrayal of Calhoun as "an architect of disaster" in an idiosyncratic exposition of the history of American democracy.

**966.** Benton, Thomas H. *Thirty Years' View; or a History of the Working of the American Government for Thirty Years, from 1820 to 1850.* 2 vols. New York: D. Appleton & Co., 1854–1856. Calhoun's career followed critically by an envious rival.

**967.** [Cunningham, Clarence, ed.] *A History of the Calhoun Monument at Charleston, S.C.* Charleston, S.C.: privately printed, 1888. Memorial speeches and tributes by Northern and Southern public figures.

**968.** Curry, J. L. M. "Principles, Acts, and Utterances of John C. Calhoun Promotive of the True Union of the States." *University of Chicago Record* 3 (July 1898): 93–112. Calhoun's efforts to preserve the Union reviewed by a postbellum Southern spokesman.

**969.** Dodd, William E. *Statesmen of the Old South, or from Radicalism to Conservative Revolt.* New York: Macmillan, 1911. Calhoun as a transitional figure between Jeffersonianism and secession.

**970.** Elliott, Edward G. "Die Staatslehre John C. Calhouns." *Staats- und-völkerrechtliche Abhandlungen* 4 (1903). Calhoun as a retarder of progress.

**971.** Hart, Albert Bushnell. *The American Triumvirate: Clay, Webster, Calhoun.* New York: Mentor Association, 1917. Conventional evaluation by a leading historian of the early 20th century.

**972.** Johnson, Gerald W. *America's Silver Age. The Statecraft of Clay, Webster, Calhoun.* New York and London: Harper & Brothers, 1939. Unsympathetic view of Calhoun in his times by a progressive Southerner.

**973.** Lodge, Henry Cabot. "John C. Calhoun." In Lodge, *The Democracy of the Constitution, and Other Essays and Addresses.* New York: Scribner's, 1915, pp. 160–185. Evaluation by a turn-of-the-century nationalist who was partly reconciled to the South.

**974.** Longacre, James B., and James Herring, eds. *The National Portrait Gallery of Distinguished Americans,* Philadelphia: Henry Perkins, 1834–1839. 4 vols. 2:13ff. A mid-career evaluation.

**975.** Longstreet, A. B. "Review of Ex. Gov. Perry's Sketch of J. C. Calhoun." *XIX Century* 2 (January 1870): 618–630. Longstreet, a lifelong acquaintance, presents his own recollections of Calhoun in the form of a criticism of Benjamin F. Perry's (#979).

**976.** Lovat-Fraser, J. A. "John Caldwell Calhoun: Another Study in Disappointment." *London Quarterly Review* 151 (April 1929): 227–238. Brief and shallow rehash of the thesis of Hermann E. von Holst's *John C. Calhoun.*

**977.** Lytle, Andrew. "John C. Calhoun." In *The Hero with the Private Parts: Essays by Andrew Lytle,* pp. 205–276. Baton Rouge, La.: Louisiana State University Press, 1966. A profound analysis of Calhoun's success and failure as a statesman marshalling an ideal pattern for the South.

**978.** Padover, Saul K. "The American as States' Righter: John C. Calhoun (1782–1850)." In Padover, *The Genius of America: Men Whose Ideas Shaped our Civilization,* pp. 138–155. New York: McGraw-Hill, 1960. A balanced review of Calhoun's place in American history.

**979.** Perry, Benjamin F. "Reminiscences of Public Men. John C. Calhoun." *XIX Century* 6 (November 1869): 417–422. (Reprinted in *The Writings of Benjamin F. Perry*. Edited by Stephen Meats and Edwin T. Arnold. 3 vols. Spartanburg, S.C.: Reprint Co., 1980, 2:72–79.) Unsympathetic recollections by a leading South Carolina "Unionist."

**980.** Pinckney, Charles C. "Calhoun from a Southern Standpoint." *Lippincott's Monthly* 62 (July 1898): 81–90.

**981.** Porter, Benjamin F. "Memoir of Hon. John C. Calhoun." In John Belton O'Neall, *Biographical Sketches of the Bench and Bar of South Carolina*, 2:289–312. Charleston, S.C.: S. G. Courtenay & Co., 1859. 2 vols. Contemporary comments by a Southern admirer.

**982.** Pritchett, John Perry. *Calhoun, His Defence of the South*. Poughkeepsie, N.Y.: printed by Harmon, 1937. Systematic analysis of Calhoun's defense of the South as a minority section in a federal republic.

**983.** Reviews of *The Papers of John C. Calhoun*, offices of the Calhoun editorial project, Columbia, S.C. Sizable collection of published reviews of volumes of *The Papers of John C. Calhoun* and other works on Calhoun, containing comments on aspects of Calhoun's career by many historians.

**984.** Rossiter, Clinton. "The Giants of American Conservatism." *American Heritage* 6 (October 1955): 56–59, 94–96. Sympathetic popular treatment of Calhoun's value in American history.

**985.** Rush, Richard. "Character of Mr. Calhoun." In Rush, *Occasional Productions, Political, Diplomatic, and Miscellaneous*, pp. 105–115. Philadelphia: J. B. Lippincott & Co., 1860. Complimentary, by a contemporary Pennsylvania politician.

**986.** Schultz, Harold. "A Century of Calhoun Biographies." *South Atlantic Quarterly* 50 (April 1951): 248–254. Survey of biographical treatment.

**987.** "Selection of Senators Whose Portraits are to be Placed in the Senate Reception Room." *Congressional Record* 103, part 5 (May 1, 1957): 6206–6208. John F. Kennedy's report on the reasons for selecting Calhoun as one of the five greatest senators.

**988.** *Statue of Hon. John C. Calhoun. Erected in Statuary Hall of the Capitol at Washington: Proceedings in Statuary Hall and in the*

*Senate and the House of Representatives on the Occasion of the Unveiling, Reception, and Acceptance of the Statue from the State of South Carolina.* Washington: Government Printing Office, 1910. Collection of commemorative and evaluative addresses.

**989.** Thomas, John L., ed. *John C. Calhoun: A Profile.* New York: Hill and Wang, 1968. A collection of interpretive articles from the nineteenth and twentieth centuries.

**990.** Trent, William Peterfield. *Southern Statesmen of the Old Regime.* Boston and New York: Thomas Y. Crowell & Co., 1897. Unsympathetic portrait by a progressive Southerner, pp. 153–193.

**991.** U.S. Congress. "Ceremonies in the Old Senate Chamber Commemorating the 200th Anniversary of the Birth of John C. Calhoun of South Carolina." *Congressional Record* 128 (March 18, 1982): S2410–S2415. Tributes and evaluations by South Carolina historians and public officials.

**992.** U.S. Senate. *Proceedings at the Unveiling of the Portraits of Five Outstanding Senators. Henry Clay . . . Daniel Webster . . . John C. Calhoun . . . Robert M. LaFollette . . . Robert A. Taft.* Washington: U.S. Government Printing Office, 1959. Documents surrounding the naming of Calhoun as one of the five great senators.

**993.** Wilson, Clyde N. "Introduction." In Wilson, *John C. Calhoun: A Bibliography* (Bibliographies of American Notables Series). Westport, Conn.: Meckler Corporation, 1990. Problems in the historical evaluation of Calhoun.

**994.** ———. Introduction to Hermann E. von Holst, *John C. Calhoun* (reprint edition), pp. xv–xxvii. New York and London: Chelsea House, 1980. Evaluation of Calhoun's career and common misunderstandings of it.

**995.** ———. "John C. Calhoun." *Research Guide to American History.* Edited by Robert Muccigrosso. Washington: Beacham Publishing Co., 1989. Overview of biographical literature, pp. 234–240.

**996.** ———. "Statesmen of the American Experiment." *The World and I* 3 (January 1988): 434–439. Common misinterpretations of Calhoun examined.

**997.** Wiltse, Charles M. "Calhoun: An Interpretation." *South Carolina Historical Association Proceedings* (1948): 26–38. Calhoun as an advocate of liberty against economic concentration and executive power in the Jacksonian era.

## B. POLITICAL THOUGHT

### 1. Monographs

**998.** Buttà, Giuseppe. *Democrazia e Federalismo: John C. Calhoun.* Messina, Italy: P & M Associati, 1988. Largely admiring study of Calhoun's political thought as relevant to the consensual aspects of democracy.

**999.** Current, Richard N. *John C. Calhoun.* New York: Washington Square Press, 1963. Sees Calhoun as a reactionary and argues the inapplicability of his ideas to later times.

**1000.** Marmor, Theodore R. *The Career of John C. Calhoun: Politician, Social Critic, Political Philosopher.* New York and London: Garland Publishing, Inc., 1988. (Harvard Dissertations in American History and Political Science series.) An original and occasionally insightful analysis of Calhoun's career measured against the ideal of republican statesmanship, agrarian thought, and Southern nationalism.

**1001.** Spain, August O. *The Political Theory of John C. Calhoun.* New York: Bookman Associates, 1951; New York: Octagon Books, 1968. The best systematic analysis of the sources and nature of Calhoun's political philosophy.

**1002.** Zeigel, Elizabeth. "The Political Philosophy of John C. Calhoun." Ph.D. dissertation, Vanderbilt University, 1932.

### 2. Short General Treatments

**1003.** Acton, Lord John. "Political Causes of the American Revolution." *The Rambler,* new series 5 (May 1861): 17–61. Calhoun's arguments combine "the realities of modern democracy" with the "securities of mediaeval freedom."

**1004.** [Bryan, Edward B.] "The Political Philosophy of South-Carolina." *Southern Quarterly Review* 23 (January 1853): 120–140. Contemporary Southern survey of Calhoun and other South Carolina thinkers.

**1005.** Clarke, James D. "Calhoun and the Concept of the 'Reactionary Enlightenment': An Examination of the Disquisition on Government." Ph.D. dissertation, University of Keele, England, 1982. "Modernist" aspects of Calhoun's thought.

**1006.** Gabriel, Ralph Henry. "A Footnote on John C. Calhoun." In Gabriel's *The Course of American Democratic Thought*, pp. 107–114. New York: Ronald Press, 1956. Argues that Calhoun "defined nationalism in terms of a satisfied and happy minority."

**1007.** [Garnett, Muscoe R. H.] "Calhoun on Government." *Southern Quarterly Review*, 23 (April 1853): 333–379. Contemporary Southern review of *A Disquisition on Government*.

**1008.** Hartz, Louis. *The Liberal Tradition in America*. New York: Harcourt, Brace & World, Inc., 1955. Sees a conflict between "Burkean traditionalism" and "Jeffersonian rationalism" in Calhoun's thought.

**1009.** Hofstadter, Richard. "John C. Calhoun: The Marx of the Master Class." In Hofstadter's *The American Political Tradition and the Men Who Made It*. New York: Alfred A. Knopf, 1948. An influential interpretation of Calhoun as an early class-conflict theorist.

**1010.** Kirk, Russell. "Southern Conservatism: Randolph and Calhoun." In Kirk's *The Conservative Mind: From Burke to Santayana*, pp. 130–160. Chicago: Henry Regnery, 1953 (and several later editions). Discussion of Calhoun and the roots and nature of Southern conservatism.

**1011.** Lerner, Ralph. "Calhoun's New Science of Politics." *American Political Science Quarterly* 57 (December 1963): 918–932. Rates Calhoun as a political innovator and regards the "concurrent majority" as an important contribution to democratic thought.

**1012.** "Life of John C. Calhoun." *Southern Quarterly Review* 3 (April 1843): 496–531. Contemporary Southern review of Calhoun's ideas in action.

**1013.** McLaughlin, Andrew C. *A Constitutional History of the United States.* New York and London: D. Appleton-Century Co., 1936. Reasonably dispassionate discussion of Calhoun's ideas in regard to several aspects of Constitutional history.

**1014.** McWilliams, Wilson C. "John Caldwell Calhoun." In *The Blackwell Encyclopedia of Political Thought.* Edited by David Miller. Oxford: Basil Blackwell, 1987, pp. 54–55. Brief and critical treatment of Calhoun's thought.

**1015.** Merriam, Charles E. "The Political Philosophy of John C. Calhoun." In *Studies in Southern History and Politics, Inscribed to William Archibald Dunning . . . by His Former Pupils the Authors,* pp. 317–338. New York: Columbia University Press, 1914. Pedestrian overview.

**1016.** Mill, John Stuart. *Considerations on Representative Government.* London: Longmans, Green, 1890. Complimentary appraisal of Calhoun's thought.

**1017.** Ogburn, Charlton. "The Constitutional Principles of John C. Calhoun." *Journal of Public Law* 2 (Fall 1953): 303–313. Slight.

**1018.** Parrington, Vernon Louis. *Main Currents in American Thought,* 3 vols. New York: Harcourt Brace, 1927. An influential interpretation of Calhoun as an exponent of "Greek democracy" (2:69–82).

**1019.** Post, C. Gordon. Introduction to Post, ed., *Calhoun: A Disquisition on Government and Selections from the Discourse,* pp. vii–xxx. Indianapolis: Bobbs-Merrill Educational Publishing, 1953. The universality of Calhoun's political thought.

**1020.** Stephenson, Nathaniel W. "Calhoun and the Divine Right of the Majority." *Scripps College Papers* 3 (March 1930): 21–38. Lectures for a series on representative Americans.

**1021.** Tozawa, Kenji. ["John C. Calhoun's Concurrent Majority."] *Ehime Law Review* 19 (January 1986): 67–95. Japanese study, refreshingly direct.

**1022.** Wilson, Clyde N. "Calhoun and Community." *Chronicles of Culture* 9 (July 1985): 17–20. The concurrent majority is not a theory of minority rights but a theory of consensus.

## 3. Background

**1023.** Atwell, Priscilla Ann. "Freedom and Diversity: Continuity in the Political Tradition of Thomas Jefferson and John C. Calhoun." Ph.D. dissertation, University of California-Los Angeles, 1967. A clear and able discussion of Calhoun's political thought from the point of view of republican theory and organicism.

**1024.** Bradford, M. E. "No Master but the Law: The Legacy of William Henry Drayton." In Bradford, *A Better Guide than Reason: Studies in the American Revolution,* pp. 111–133. LaSalle, Ill.: Sherwood Sugden & Co., 1979. The political thought of a South Carolina Revolutionary jurist sheds light on Calhoun's constitutional understanding.

**1025.** ———. "Preserving the Birthright: The Intention of South Carolina in Adopting the U.S. Constitution." *South Carolina Historical Magazine* 89 (April 1988): 90–101. The motivations and understandings of South Carolina in ratifying the Constitution.

**1026.** ———. "A Teaching for Republicans: Roman History and the Nation's First Identity." In Bradford, *A Better Guide than Reason: Studies in the American Revolution,* pp. 3–27. LaSalle, Ill.: Sherwood Sugden & Co., 1979. Roman influences on Southern republicanism.

**1027.** Calhoon, Robert M. *Evangelicals and Conservatives in the Early South, 1740–1861.* Columbia, S.C.: University of South Carolina Press, 1988. Important study of the relationship of Southern religious and political thought in Calhoun's era.

**1028.** Carpenter, Jesse T. *The South as a Conscious Minority, 1789–1861.* New York: New York University Press, 1930. Classic study of Southern constitutional defenses.

**1029.** Harp, Gillis J. "Taylor, Calhoun, and the Decline of a Theory of Political Disharmony." *Journal of the History of Ideas* 66 (January–March 1965): 107–120. Calhoun and John Taylor of Caroline.

**1030.** Hill, C. William. "Contrasting Themes in the Political Theories of Jefferson, Calhoun, and John Taylor of Caroline." *Publius* 6 (Summer 1976): 73–92.

**1031.** Kateb, George. "The Majority Principle: Calhoun and His Antecedents." *Political Science Quarterly* 84 (December 1969): 583–605. Anti-majoritarianism in American tradition.

**1032.** Senese, Donald J. "Legal Thought in South Carolina, 1800–1860." Ph.D. dissertation, University of South Carolina, 1970. Portrait of philosophical rather than pragmatic legal conservatism.

**1033.** Shalhope, Robert E. "Republicanism and Early American Historiography." *William and Mary Quarterly* 39 (April 1982): 334–356. With the two following, indispensable background to Calhoun's thought.

**1034.** ———. "Thomas Jefferson's Republicanism and Antebellum Southern Thought." *Journal of Southern History* 42 (November 1976): 529–556.

**1035.** ———. "Toward a Republican Synthesis: The Emergence of an Understanding of Republicanism in American Historiography." *William and Mary Quarterly* 29 (January 1972): 49–80.

**1036.** Smiley, David L. "Revolutionary Origins of the South's Constitutional Defenses." *North Carolina Historical Review* 44 (July 1965): 256–269.

**1037.** Walker, Mary M. "Problems of Majority Rule in the Political Thought of James Madison and John C. Calhoun." Ph.D. dissertation, Indiana University, 1971.

**1038.** Weir, Robert M. "South Carolinians and the Adoption of the United States Constitution." *South Carolina Historical Magazine* 89 (April 1988): 73–89. South Carolina's understanding of the powers and purposes of the federal government at the time of ratification of the Constitution.

**1039.** Wilson, Clyde N. "Introduction to Two Special Issues: South Carolina and the U.S. Constitution." *South Carolina Historical Magazine* 89 (April 1988): 69–72. South Carolina's unique and critical relationship to the history of the Constitution.

**1040.** Wiltse, Charles M. "From Compact to National State in American Political Thought." In *Essays in Political Theory Presented to George H. Sabine,* pp. 153–178. Ithaca, N.Y.: Cornell University Press, 1948. Calhoun's defense of the compact theory of the Union in the context of the movement of American political thought from the rights of man to sovereign national power.

**1041.** Wood, Walter K. "The Union of the States: A Study of Radical Whig-Republican Ideology and Its Influence upon the Nation and the

South, 1776–1861." Ph.D. dissertation, University of South Carolina, 1978. The intellectual background of states rights doctrine.

## 4. Contemporary and Later Defences of States Rights

**1042.** Baldwin, Henry. *A General View of the Origin and Nature of the Constitution and Government of the United States, Deduced from the Political History and Condition of the Colonies and States, from 1774 until 1788, and the Decisions of the Supreme Court; with Opinions in the Cases Decided at January Term 1837, Arising on the Restraints on the Powers of the States.* Philadelphia: John C. Clark, 1837. By a Supreme Court justice from Pennsylvania.

**1043.** Berger, Raoul. *Federalism: Evaluating the Founders' Design.* Norman, Okla.: University of Oklahoma Press, 1987. A modern partial revival of states rights by a judicial scholar.

**1044.** Bledsoe, Albert Taylor. *Is Davis a Traitor; or Was Secession a Constitutional Right Previous to the War of 1861?* Baltimore: Innes & Co., 1866. Probably the most powerful of the Southern arguments for state sovereignty.

**1045.** Dabney, Robert L. *A Defence of Virginia and through Her of the South in Recent and Pending Contests against the Sectional Party.* New York: E. J. Hale & Son, 1867.

**1046.** Davis, Jefferson. *Rise and Fall of the Confederate Government.* 2 vols. New York: D. Appleton & Co., 1881.

**1047.** Garnett, Muscoe R. H. *The Union, Past and Future: How it Works and How to Save It.* Charleston, S.C.: Walker & James, 1850.

**1048.** Gildersleeve, Basil L. *The Creed of the Old South, 1865–1915.* Baltimore: Johns Hopkins Press, 1915.

**1049.** Rawle, William. *A View of the Constitution of the United States.* Philadelphia: Carey & Lea, 1825, and later editions.

**1050.** Stephens, Alexander H. *A Constitutional View of the Late War Between the States.* 2 vols. Philadelphia: National Publishing Co., 1868, 1870.

**1051.** Tucker, John Randolph. *The Constitution of the United States.* Chicago: Callaghan & Co., 1899.

**1052.** Upshur, Abel P. *A Brief Enquiry into the True Nature and Character of Our Federal Government: Being a Review of Judge Story's Commentaries on the Constitution of the United States.* Petersburg, Va.: 1840; Philadelphia: J. Campbell, 1863.

## 5. Economics

**1053.** Buttà, Giuseppe. "Politica, economica e societa nel penserios di John C. Calhoun." *Historica* 34 (January–March 1981): 3–8. Complimentary as to the value of Calhoun's thought in the problem of balancing economic interests.

**1054.** Donoghue, Francis J. "The Economic and Social Principles of John C. Calhoun." Ph.D. dissertation, Columbia University, 1969. A neglected study which is by far the best treatment of Calhoun's economics, both factual and interpretive.

**1055.** Dorfman, Joseph. *The Economic Mind in American Civilization, 1606–1865.* 2 vols. New York: Viking Press, 1946. Calhoun appears *passim.*

**1056.** Ford, Lacy K. "Recovering the Republic: Calhoun, South Carolina, and the Concurrent Majority." *South Carolina Historical Magazine* 89 (July 1988): 146–159. Calhoun's revision of Madison's "faction" theory: rather than militating against a coherent majority, factions tend to combine until they achieve an exploitive majority combination.

**1057.** ———. "Republican Ideology in a Slave Society: The Political Economy of John C. Calhoun." *Journal of Southern History* 54 (August 1988): 405–424. Calhoun and the "American System."

**1058.** [Green, Benjamin E.] *Opinions of John C. Calhoun and Thomas Jefferson on the Subject of Paper Currency.* [No publisher: no date]. A Greenback era analysis of Calhoun's monetary views.

**1059.** Green, Ben E. "Translator's Preface." In Adolphe Granier de Cassagnac, *History of the Working and Burgher Classes.* Philadelphia: Claxton, Remsen & Haffelfinger, 1871. Ben Green makes use of Calhoun's ideas on class conflict and currency for a "Greenback" argument.

**1060.** Marmor, Theodore R. "Anti-Industrialism and the Old South: The Agrarian Perspective of John C. Calhoun." *Comparative Studies in Society and History* 9 (1967): 377–406. Calhoun as economic liberal and antimercantilist.

**1061.** Prentice, E. Parmalee. "John C. Calhoun and the Labor Question." *Harvard Law Review* 14 (May 1900): 44–51.

**1062.** Taussig, Frank W. *The Tariff History of the United States.* New York: G. P. Putnam's Sons, 1925. Standard.

## 6. Slavery

**1063.** Bartlett, Irving H. *The American Mind in the Mid-Nineteenth Century.* New York: Thomas Y. Crowell, 1967. Brief, cogent overview of Calhoun's thought in defense of slavery (pp. 80–86).

**1064.** Binney, Charles C. *The Life of Horace Binney, with Selections from His Letters.* Philadelphia and London: J. B. Lippincott Co., 1903. Recollection of 1834 conversation between Calhoun and a Philadelphia theologian in which Calhoun spoke of Southern slavery and impending class conflict in the North (pp. 133–136).

**1065.** Boller, Paul F., Jr. "Calhoun on Liberty." *South Atlantic Quarterly* 66 (Summer 1967): 395–408. From Lockean liberty to defense of slavery.

**1066.** ———. "John C. Calhoun on Liberty as Privilege." In Boller, *Freedom and Fate in American Thought from Edwards to Dewey,* pp. 81–105. Dallas: Southern Methodist University Press, 1978. Expanded version of preceding.

**1067.** Carsel, Wilfred. "The Slaveholders' Indictment of Northern Wage Slavery." *Journal of Southern History* 6 (November 1940): 504–520.

**1068.** Fitzhugh, George. "The Politics and Economics of Aristotle and Mr. Calhoun." *DeBow's Review* 23 (August 1857): 163–172. Critical discussion of Calhoun's *A Disquisition on Government* by a defender of slavery.

**1069.** Garson, Robert A. "Proslavery as Political Theory: The Examples of John C. Calhoun and George Fitzhugh." *South Atlantic Quarterly* 84 (Spring 1965): 197–212.

**1070.** Genovese, Eugene D. *The World the Slaveholders Made: Two Essays in Interpretation.* New York: Pantheon Books, 1969; revised edition, Middletown, Conn.: Wesleyan University Press, 1988. The development of a proslavery philosophy by Calhoun's contemporaries.

**1071.** Gliddon, George R., and Josiah C. Nott. *Types of Mankind: or Ethnological Researches* . . . Philadelphia: Lippincott, Grambo & Co., 1854. Gliddon was a Philadelphian who had spent much time in Africa. (Conversations with Calhoun, pp. 50–52.)

**1072.** Jenkins, William Sumner. *Pro-Slavery Thought in the Old South.* Chapel Hill, N.C.: University of North Carolina Press, 1935. Classic study.

**1073.** [Musson, Eugène.] *Lettre à Napoléon III sur l'esclavage aux états du Sud, par un Créole de la Louisiane.* Paris: Dentu, 1862. A defense of slavery by a Louisianan, based largely on Calhoun's speeches and writings.

**1074.** Wiesen, David S. "The Contributions of Antiquity to American Racial Thought." In *Classical Traditions in Early America.* Edited by John W. Eadie. Ann Arbor, Mich.: University of Michigan Center for Coordination of Ancient and Modern Studies, 1976, pp. 191–212.

**1075.** Wilson, Clyde N. "John Caldwell Calhoun." In Randall M. Miller and John David Smith, eds., *The Dictionary of Afro-American Slavery.* Westport, Conn.: Greenwood Press, 1988. Succinct account of Calhoun's relationship to slavery, personal and political (pp. 93–94).

**1076.** Wiltshire, Susan F. "Jefferson, Calhoun, and the Slavery Debate: The Classics and the Two Minds of the South." *Southern Humanities Review* 11 (1977): 33–40.

## 7. Miscellany

**1077.** Buttà, Giuseppe. "John C. Calhoun, Tocqueville e la rivoluzione del '48 in Francia e in Germania." *Iustitua* 33 (April-June 1980): 97–121. Calhoun's response to the European revolutions of 1848.

**1078.** Coleman, Frank J. *Hobbes and America: Exploring the Constitutional Foundations.* Toronto: University of Toronto Press, 1977. Contains a chapter on "Madison, Thoreau, Calhoun, and Sumner" (pp. 121–147).

**1079.** Curti, Merle E. "John C. Calhoun and the Unification of Germany." *American Historical Review* 40 (April 1935): 476.

**1080.** Dunning, William A. *A History of Political Theory: From Rousseau to Spencer.* New York: Macmillan, 1920. Brief but illuminating discussion of Calhoun's concept of sovereignty compared with various German thinkers.

**1081.** Freehling, William W. "Spoilsmen and Interests in the Thought and Career of John C. Calhoun." *Journal of American History* 52 (June 1965): 25–42. Finds Calhoun an economic determinist but an inconsistent one because he was "unable to decide whether pressure groups or politicians caused historical events."

**1082.** Harris, J. William. "Last of the Classical Republicans: An Interpretation of John C. Calhoun." *Civil War History* 30 (September 1984): 255–267. Calhoun as a Renaissance republican.

**1083.** Heckscher, Gunnar. "Calhoun's Idea of the Concurrent Majority and the Constitutional Theory of Hegel." *American Political Science Review* 33 (August 1939): 585–590.

**1084.** Mitchell, Franklin. "The Roman Origin and the American Justification of the Tribunital or Veto Power in the Charter of the United Nations." *Tulane Law Review* 22 (October 1947): 24–61. First noted the applicability of the concurrent majority to international organizations.

**1085.** Moltmann, Gunter. "Amerikanische Beitrage Zur Deutschen VerfassungsDiskussion 1848." *Jahrbuch fur Amerikastudien* 12 (1967): 206–226. Contributions of American thinkers, including Calhoun, to the German constitutional debate of 1848.

**1086.** Thatcher, Harold W. "Calhoun and Federal Reinforcement of State Laws." *American Political Science Review* 36 (October 1942): 873–880.

**1087.** White, Laura A. "The Fate of Calhoun's Sovereign Convention in South Carolina." *American Historical Review* 34 (July 1929): 757–771. Problems in the application of state sovereignty.

**1088.** Wiltse, Charles M. "A Critical Southerner: John C. Calhoun on the Revolutions of 1848." *Journal of Southern History* 15 (August 1949): 299–310.

**1089.** Zwicker, Dietrich. *Der Amerikanische Staatsman John C. Calhoun, ein Kämpfer gegen die "Ideen von 1789."* Vaduz: Kraus Reprint Co., 1965. (Originally published Berlin, 1935). Calhoun and the French Revolution.

## C. TWENTIETH-CENTURY APPLICATIONS

**1090.** Amacher, Anne W. "Myths and Consequences: Calhoun and Some Nashville Agrarians." *South Atlantic Quarterly* 59 (Spring 1960): 251–264. The alleged use of Calhoun as a prophet and messiah of a feudal order is dubious.

**1091.** Ball, William Watts. *Essays in Reaction: Back to Calhoun; Back to Aristocracy.* Columbia, S.C.: privately printed, 1925. A leading South Carolina newspaper editor applies Calhounian principles to early 20th century state politics.

**1092.** Barr, James Madison. "John C. Calhoun's Concurrent Majority." *Human Events* 19 (January 13, 1962): 25–27. Complimentary reflections on the importance of the concurrent majority, though written under the debatable impression that Calhoun was a Unitarian.

**1093.** Baskin, Darryl. "The Pluralist Vision of John C. Calhoun." *Polity* 2 (Fall 1969): 49–65. Condemns the concurrent majority as a mechanical and inadequate idea of the public interest.

**1094.** Bradford, M. E. "Where We Were Born and Raised: On the Continuity of Southern Conservatism." *Southern Review* 25 (Spring 1989): 334–350. Calhoun and the Declaration of Independence.

**1095.** Coit, Margaret L. "Calhoun and the Downfall of States' Rights." *Virginia Quarterly Review* 28 (Spring 1952): 191–208. Analysis of Calhoun's ideas in regard to the political situation of the early 1950s.

**1096.** Current, Richard N. "John C. Calhoun: Philosopher of Reaction." *Antioch Review* 3 (Summer 1943): 223–234. Sees Calhoun as the architect and presiding spirit of reactionary coalitions in the twentieth century.

**1097.** Drucker, Peter F. "A Key to American Politics: Calhoun's Pluralism." *Review of Politics* 10 (October 1948): 412–426. Calhoun seen as the first to discern the centrality of "pluralism" to democratic politics.

**1098.** Elwell, Margaret Coit. "The Continuing Relevance of John C. Calhoun." *Continuity: A Journal of History* 9 (Fall 1984): 73–85. The perennial relevance of Calhoun's thought to conditions in the twentieth century.

**1099.** Faulkner, Ronnie W. "Taking John C. Calhoun to the United Nations." *Polity* 15 (Summer 1983): 473–491. How the UN Charter reflects the concurrent majority.

**1100.** Faulkner, Ronnie W., and Michael M. Gunter. "UN Ambassador Daniel Patrick Moynihan and the Calhounian Connection." *Teaching Political Science: Politics in Perspective* 13 (Winter 1985–1986): 68–81. Finds Moynihan's analysis of the United States' minority status in the UN similar to Calhoun's thought.

**1101.** Fischer, John. "Unwritten Rules of American Politics." *Harper's Magazine* 197 (November 1948): 27–36. The concurrent majority discovered to provide the best description of the American political tradition.

**1102.** Fleming, Thomas. *The Politics of Human Nature.* New Brunswick, N.J., and Oxford: Transaction Books, 1988. Calhoun figures in a chapter on "The Federal Principle" in human nature.

**1103.** Hollis, Christopher. *The American Heresy.* London: Sheed & Ward, 1927; New York: Minton, Balch, 1930. An English writer treats Jefferson, Calhoun, Lincoln, and Wilson as the great figures in forming the American way (pp. 99–169).

**1104.** Jeffrey, Robert C. "The Thought of John C. Calhoun: The Key to the Liberal Critique of American Politics." Ph.D. dissertation, University of Dallas, 1985. Eccentric exercise of the Straussian political science school, lacking historical perspective.

**1105.** Kirk, Russell. "Calhoun Endures." *Southern Partisan* 9 (Third Quarter 1989): 20–24. Calhoun will survive the shallow attacks of contemporary critics and maintain his importance as a premier American political thinker.

**1106.** Kuic, Vukan. "John C. Calhoun's Theory of the 'Concurrent Majority.'" *American Bar Association Journal* 69 (April 1983): 482–486. An argument for the continued applicability of the "concurrent majority" as seen in recent judicial decisions.

**1107.** Longman, Phillip. "From Calhoun to Sister Boom-Boom: The Dubious Legacy of Interest Group Politics." *Washington Monthly* 15 (June 1983): 11–22. Strangely blames Calhoun for modern interest-group politics.

**1108.** Morley, Felix. *Freedom and Federalism*. Chicago: Henry Regnery, 1951. Complimentary treatment of Calhoun's relevance to the American situation of the mid-twentieth century.

**1109.** ———. "Progress Turns on Rivalry of Ideas." *Nation's Business* 43 (October 1953): 17–18. Conflict of ideas between Calhoun and John Marshall.

**1110.** "Negative Power." *Time*, May 19, 1952, pp. 29–32. The concurrent majority expressed in 1950s Southern political strategy.

**1111.** Potter, David M. *The South and the Concurrent Majority*. Baton Rouge, La.: Louisiana State University Press, 1972. The concurrent majority through twentieth century American history.

**1112.** Rogers, George C., Jr. "A Southern Political Tradition." In *Why the South Will Survive, by Fifteen Southerners*. Edited by Clyde N. Wilson, pp. 81–90. Athens, Ga.: University of Georgia Press, 1981. Applications to modern problems.

**1113.** Röpke, Wilhelm. *The Social Crisis of Our Time*. Chicago: University of Chicago Press, 1950. (Originally published in German, 1942.) Calhoun treated as a useful authority on twentieth century problems.

**1114.** Rossiter, Clinton. *Conservatism in America*. New York: Alfred A. Knopf, 1955. The concurrent majority lives on in America in many "techniques and arrangements" (pp. 122–126).

**1115.** Ryn, Claes G. *Democracy and the Ethical Life: A Philosophy of Politics and Community*. Baton Rouge, La., and London: Louisiana State University Press, 1978. Calhoun on constitutionalism as a moral necessity (pp. 168–177).

**1116.** Schlesinger, Arthur M., Jr. "Calhoun Restored." *The Nation* 170 (April 1, 1950): 302. Time to consider Calhoun's relevance to the present.

**1117.** Steinberger, Peter J. "Calhoun's Concept of the Public Interest: A Clarification." *Polity* 13 (Spring 1981): 410–424. Calhoun's views of self-interest considered in relation to those of the American founders and various European thinkers.

**1118.** Walton, Hanes. *The Political Philosophy of Martin Luther King, Jr.* Westport, Conn.: Greenwood Press, 1971. Calhoun's concurrent majority explicitly applied to the political representation of racial minorities.

**1119.** White, William S. *Citadel: The Story of the U.S. Senate.* New York: Harper & Brothers, 1956. A twentieth-century reporter on Calhoun's role in the shaping of the Senate as an institution.

**1120.** Wilson, Clyde N. "Calhoun and the Constitution: Some Bicentennial Reflections." *Carologue* (South Carolina Historical Society newsletter), September-October 1987: 8–13. Argues for Calhoun's relevance to the understanding of the Constitution.

**1121.** Wiltse, Charles M. "Calhoun and the Modern State." *Virginia Quarterly Review* 13 (Summer 1937): 396–408. Applications of Calhoun's thought to economic conflict in the twentieth century.

**1122.** ———. "Calhoun's Democracy." *Journal of Politics* 3 (May 1941): 210–223. Relevance of Calhoun's thought to the twentieth century.

**1123.** Worsthorne, Peregrine. "John C. Calhoun." *Encounter* 5 (July 1955): 63–70. Calhoun as "one of the truly prophetic political thinkers of American history."

## D. ORATORICAL AND LITERARY ANALYSIS

**1124.** "American Oratory." *Southern Quarterly Review* 5 (April 1844): 361–391. Contemporary review of *Speeches of John C. Calhoun.*

**1125.** Anderson, James L., and W. Edwin Hemphill. "The 1843 Biography of John C. Calhoun: Was Robert M. T. Hunter Its Author?" *Journal of Southern History* 38 (August 1972): 470–474. Lays to rest the charge that the 1843 biography was a clandestine autobiography. (See # 1140)

**1126.** Bass, Robert D. "An Autobiography of William John Grayson, Edited with an Introduction." Ph.D. dissertation, University of South Carolina, 1933. Memoirs of a South Carolina literary contemporary, especially good on Calhoun's style (pp. 212–213).

**1127.** Benoit, William Lyon, and Alexander Moore. "John C. Calhoun (1782–1850), Spokesperson for the South and the Union." In Bernard K. Duffy and Halford R. Ryan, *American Orators before 1900: Critical Studies and Sources*, pp. 68–78. New York and other places: Greenwood Press, 1987. Overview of Calhoun's rhetoric with bibliography to a sizable specialized speech literature on Calhoun.

**1128.** Bradley, Bert E. "John C. Calhoun's Rhetorical Method in Defense of Slavery." In Waldo W. Braden, ed., *Oratory in the Old South, 1828–1860*. Baton Rouge, La.: Louisiana State University Press, 1970.

**1129.** ———. "Refutative Techniques of John C. Calhoun." *Southern Speech Communication Journal* 37 (Summer 1972): 413–423.

**1130.** Bradley, Bert E., and Jerry L. Tarver. "John C. Calhoun's Argumentation in Defence of Slavery." *Southern Speech Communication Journal* 35 (Winter 1969): 163–175.

**1131.** [Brownson, Orestes A.] "Life and Speeches of John C. Calhoun." *Brownson's Quarterly Review* 1 (January 1844): 105–131. View of a contemporary Northern admirer of Calhoun.

**1132.** "Characteristics of the Statesman." *Southern Quarterly Review* 6 (July 1844): 95–129. Contemporary Southern comparison of Calhoun's oratory with that of Henry Clay and others.

**1133.** Curry, Herbert L. "An Evaluation of the Debating Techniques of John Caldwell Calhoun in Representative Pro-Slavery Speeches, 1847–1850." M.A. thesis, State University of Iowa, 1936.

**1134.** ———. "John C. Calhoun." In William N. Brigance, ed., *A History and Criticism of American Public Address*, 2:639–664. New York: Russell and Russell, 1960, 3 vols. Analysis of Calhoun's speechmaking.

**1135.** Downs, Robert B. *Books that Changed the South*. Chapel Hill, N.C.: University of North Carolina Press, 1977. The *Disquisition on Government,* pp. 103–113.

**1136.** Eubanks, Ralph T. "The Rhetoric of the Nullifiers." In Waldo W. Braden, ed., *Oratory in the Old South, 1828–1860*. Baton Rouge, La.: Louisiana State University Press, 1970.

**1137.** [Garnett, Muscoe R. H.] "Life and Speeches of John C. Calhoun." *Southern Quarterly Review* 9 (January 1846): 204–236. Contemporary treatment.

**1138.** Godwin, Parke. *Out of the Past: Critical and Literary Papers*. New York: G. P. Putnam & Sons, 1870. Analysis of Calhoun's style and thought in comparison with other American statesmen (pp. 234–241).

**1139.** Hubbell, Jay B. *The South in American Literature, 1607–1900*. Durham, N.C.: Duke University Press, 1954. Judicious overview of Calhoun's intellectual processes (pp. 413–424, 922–923).

**1140.** Hunt, Gaillard, ed. "Rhett on the Biography of Calhoun, 1854." In *American Historical Review* 13 (January 1908): 310–312. Presents the thesis that Hunter's 1843 biography of Calhoun was actually a clandestine autobiography. (See # 1125)

**1141.** McLaughlin, Andrew C. "Publicists and Orators, 1800–1850." In William P. Trent et al., eds., *The Cambridge History of American Literature,* 2:70–91. New York: Macmillan, 1917–1921, 3 vols. Judicious treatment of the elements of Calhoun's speeches of interest to later generations (pp. 78–84).

**1142.** Magoon, E. L. *Living Orators in America*. New York: Baker and Scribner, 1849. Devotes a chapter to Calhoun based on first-hand observation.

**1143.** Ritzman, Carl H. "A Critical Study of Four Representative Speeches on State Rights by John C. Calhoun." M.A. thesis, State University of Iowa, 1935.

**1144.** Spiller, Robert E., et al., eds. *Literary History of the United States,* 3 vols. New York: Macmillan, 1948. Oratorical evaluation (1:551–553).

**1145.** Volpe, Michael. "The Logic of Calhoun's Constitutional Theory." *Southern Speech Communication Journal* 39 (Winter 1973): 161–172.

**1146.** [Wharton, Francis]. "Mr. Calhoun's Parliamentary Eloquence." *United States Magazine and Democratic Review* 14 (February 1844): 111–130. Views of a contemporary Northern admirer.

**1147.** White, Henry A. "John Caldwell Calhoun." In Edwin A. Alderman and Joel Chandler Harris, eds., *Library of Southern Literature*, 2:673–710. Atlanta: Martin and Hoyt, 1908–1913, 16 vols. Admiring Southern evaluation.

**1148.** Wilson, Clyde N. Introduction to Wilson, ed., *The Papers of John C. Calhoun*, vol. 12, *1833–1835*, pp. ix–xliv. Columbia, S.C.: University of South Carolina Press, 1979. Analyzes Calhoun's Senatorial oratory, post-nullification stands, and personal life.

**1149.** Winn, Larry James. "The War Hawks' Call to Arms: Appeals for a Second War with Great Britain." *Southern Speech Communication Journal* 37 (Summer 1972): 402–412.

# IX.
# Iconography

### A. PORTRAITS

**1150.** *American Library Association Portrait Index.* Washington: U.S. Government Printing Office, 1906. Listing of published engravings and other likenesses, pp. 235–236.

**1151.** Cosentino, Andrew F. *The Paintings of Charles Bird King (1785–1862).* Washington: Smithsonian Institution Press, 1977. Reproduction and description of several early Calhoun portraits.

**1152.** National Portrait Gallery, Smithsonian Institution. *Permanent Collection Illustrated Checklist.* Washington: Smithsonian Institution, 1978. Collection of Calhoun portraits described and reproduced (pp. 25–26).

**1153.** *The Papers of John C. Calhoun* picture files. Editorial offices, University of South Carolina. Sizable quantity of reproductions and unorganized research notes related to portraits and other likenesses of Calhoun.

**1154.** Rutledge, Anna Wells. "Likenesses of John C. Calhoun." Unpublished portrait catalog, South Caroliniana Library, University of South Carolina.

### B. DAGUERREOTYPES

**1155.** Ketchum, Richard M. "Faces from the Past—XXII." *American Heritage* 18 (October 1967): 18–19. The Brady likeness of Calhoun.

1156. Pfister, Harold Francis. *Facing the Light: Historic American Portrait Daguerreotypes.* Washington: Smithsonian Institution, 1978. Description and reproduction of Calhoun images (pp. 206–209, 302–303).

1157. Thorpe, Thomas B. "Webster, Clay, Calhoun, and Jackson. How They Sat for Their Daguerreotypes." *Harper's New Monthly Magazine* 38 (May 1869): 787–789.

## C. SCULPTURE

1158. "Clark Mills and His Equestrian Statue." *De Bow's Review* 16 (January 1854): 38–46. Discusses Mills's creation of his bust of Calhoun.

1159. Craven, Wayne, ed. *Sculpture in America.* Newark, Del.: University of Delaware Press, 1984. Basic information on statues and busts of Calhoun.

1160. Fuller, Margaret. "Shipwreck, Loss of Life and of Power's Statue of Calhoun." *Boston Post,* July 23, 1850. Account of the shipwreck in which Hiram Powers's statue of Calhoun was lost in the Atlantic.

1161. [Porcher, Frederick A.] "Modern Art—Powers' Statue of Calhoun." *Southern Quarterly Review*, new series, 5 (January 1852): 86–114. Art criticism by a South Carolina scholar.

1162. "[Hiram] Powers' Bust of Calhoun." *Antiques* 71 (February 1957): 175.

## D. MISCELLANY

1163. Brown, William H. *Portrait Gallery of Distinguished American Citizens, with Biographical Sketches and Fac-Similes of Original Letters.* Hartford, Conn.: E. B. and E. C. Kellogg, 1845. A silhouette of Calhoun.

1164. Criswell, Grover C., Jr. *Confederate and Southern State Bonds.* Iola, Wisc.: Krause Publications, n.d.

# Iconography

**1165.** ———. *Confederate and Southern State Currency.* Iola, Wisc.: Krause Publications, n.d. Reproductions of Calhoun images on currency.

**1166.** ———. *North American Currency. The Standard Paper Money Reference.* Iola, Wisc.: Krause Publications, n.d. Reproduction of Calhoun images on Southern bank notes.

**1167.** Hutton, Lawrence. "A Collection of Death-Masks." *Harper's New Monthly Magazine* 85 (November 1892): 904–916. Discussion and reproduction of Clark Mills's life mask of Calhoun.

**1168.** McBride, Van Dyk. "John Drinkwater's Poem about a Confederate Stamp." *Manuscripts* 6 (Fall 1953): 177–178. History of the Confederate one-cent stamp with Calhoun's likeness.

**1169.** Nevins. Allan, and Frank Weitenkampf. *A Century of Political Cartoons: Caricature in the United States from 1800 to 1900.* New York: Octagon Books, 1975. Several Calhoun entries as well as much more on his contemporaries.

**1170.** Seymour, Charles. "The New Colleges at Yale." *Yale Literary Magazine* 95 (November 1931): 10–21. Description of Yale's Calhoun College.

# X.
# Prospective Works

A few works in progress and substantially advanced but not completed in time for inclusion in this book.

**1171.** Bartlett, Irving H. A new biography of Calhoun, with much fresh material.

**1172.** Hizer, Trenton. John C. Calhoun's Early Nationalism. M.A. thesis, University of South Carolina.

**1173.** Richards, Miles S. Duff Green's Free Trade Mission to Europe. Ph.D. dissertation, University of South Carolina.

**1174.** Tozawa, Kenji. Ehime University, Japan. A book-length study of Calhoun's life and ideas.

**1175.** Wilson, Clyde N. "John C. Calhoun." Book-length study of Calhoun's political thought for the American Political Thought series, University Press of Kansas.

**1176.** Wilson, Clyde N., ed. "The Papers of John C. Calhoun," vol. 21, "1845." The consummation of Texas annexation and Calhoun's life out of office during most of the year.

# XI.
# Indexes

## AUTHOR INDEX

Abel, Annie H., 568
Acton, John E. E. D. (Lord), 1003
Adams, Charles Francis, 142
Adams, Ephraim D., 731
Adams, Henry, 519
Adams, John Quincy, 142
Adams, Porter H., 532
Adams, Randolph G., 718
Aderman, Ralph M., 99
Alexander, Holmes, 397, 826
Alley, Felix E., 941
Allston, Robert F. W., 143
Amacher, Anne W., 1090
Ambler, Charles Henry, 137, 151, 513
Ambrose, Stephen E., 555
American Library Association, 1150
Ames, Herman V., 623, 771
Ammon, Harry, 537, 538
Anderson, James L., 1125
Anderson, John M., 215
Anonymous, 408, 413, 415, 435, 534, 551, 599, 619, 678, 702, 703, 707, 708, 734, 898, 908, 909, 918, 921, 923, 924, 943, 946, 1012, 1110, 1124, 1132, 1158, 1162
Armas, Juan Ignacio de, 216
Ashley, James M., 964
Atwater, Caleb, 949
Atwell, Priscilla Ann, 1023

Bacot, D. Huger, 421
Bailey, Louise N., 488, 491
Bailey, Thomas A., 719

Baker, Elizabeth F., 833
Baldwin, Henry, 1042
Ball, William Watts, 1091
Bancroft, Frederic, 648
Barber, John Warner, 431
Barker, Eugene C., 154
Barnwell, John, 772
Barr, James Madison, 1092
Barsness, Richard W., 556
Bartlett, Irving H., 831, 832, 1063, 1171
Barton, William E., 942
Baskin, Darryl, 1093
Basler, Roy P., 158
Bass, Robert D., 1126
Bassett, John Spencer, 138, 815
Basso, Hamilton, 965
Bates, Mary, 894
Bell, John R., 580
Bell, William Gardner, 544
Belohlavek, John M., 814
Bemis, Samuel Flagg, 718, 720, 728, 803, 804
Benoit, William Lyon, 1127
Benton, Thomas Hart, 223, 966
Berger, Raoul, 1043
Bergeron, Paul H., 649, 650, 762
Biddle, Nicholas, 144
Binney, Charles C., 1064
Birdsall, C. M., 934
Bledsoe, Albert Taylor, 1044
Bleser, Carol K., 153
Bloom, John Porter, 90

Boatright, Sherry L., 935
Boller, Paul F., Jr., 1065, 1066
Boucher, Chauncey S., 27, 489, 501, 651, 732, 773
Bourne, Edward G., 684
Bourne, Kenneth, 94
Bowers, Claude G., 615
Bowie, Alexander, 452
Boyd, Jesse W., 750
Braden, Waldo W., 1128, 1136
Bradford, Gamaliel, 895
Bradford, M. E., 1024, 1025, 1026, 1094
Bradley, Bert E., 1128, 1129, 1130
Brant, Irving, 520
Brasington, George F., 652
Brauer, Kinley, 721
Breese, Donald H., 774
Bridgeforth, Lucie Robertson, 653
Brigance, William N., 1134
Briggs, Lillian M., 220
Brooks, Robert P., 27
Brown, Richard H., 605
Brown, Thomas, 674
Brown, William Garrott, 468
Brown, William H., 1163
Brownson, Henry F., 31, 873
Brownson, Orestes A., 145, 206, 207, 701, 873, 1131
Bruns, Roger, 606
Bryan, Edward B., 1004
Bryan, T. Conn, 936
Buchanan, James, 146
Burke, Pauline W., 616
Burton, Orville Vernon, 507
Butler, C. M., 796
Buttà, Giuseppe, 998, 1053, 1077
Butterworth, Keen, 866

Calhoon, Robert M., 1027
Calhoun, John C., 215–383
Calhoun, Orval A., 409
Campbell, John A., 791
Capers, Gerald M., 384, 654
Carpenter, Jesse T., 1028
Carsel, Wilfred, 1067
Carson, James Petigru, 858
Carter, Clarence E., 90
"Cassius", 585
Catlin, George, 569
Catterall, Ralph H., 533
Chambers, William Nisbet, 806

Chappell, Buford S., 902
Chesnutt, David R., 482
Chitwood, Oliver Perry, 713
Clark, Victor S., 455
Clark, W. A., 502
Clarke, James D., 1005
Clay, Henry, 147, 148, 220, 796
Cleveland, John B., 33
Clower, George Wesley, 410
Coclanis, Peter A., 503
Coit, Margaret L., 385, 426, 896, 1095, 1098
Cole, Donald B., 827
Coleman, Frank M., 1078
Colton, Calvin, 148
Cook, Harriet Hefner, 897
Cook, Harvey T., 872
Cooper, Thomas, 624
Cooper, William J., Jr., 469, 470
Corbett, Percy E., 751
Corwin, Edwin S., 631
Cosentino, Andrew F., 1151
Coulter, E. Merton, 655
Coussons, John S., 490
Crallé, Richard K., 141, 182, 217, 218, 219, 311, 314, 733, 752
Craven, Avery O., 456
Craven, Delle Mullen, 915
Craven, Wayne, 1159
Crawford, William H., 149
Criswell, Grover C., 1164, 1165, 1166
Cumming, Joseph Bryan, 586
Cunliffe, Marcus, 457
Cunningham, Clarence, 967
Current, Richard N., 398, 999, 1096
Curry, Herbert L., 1133, 1134
Curry, J. L. M., 950, 968
Curry, Roy W., 892
Curti, Merle E., 763, 1079
Curtis, George T., 809
Cutler, E. Wayne, 162, 587

Dabney, Robert Lewis, 1045
Dallas, George M., 588
Dangerfield, George, 539
Darling, Arthur B., 514
Davids, Jules, 97
Davidson, Chalmers G., 508
Davis, Curtis Carroll, 34
Davis, Jefferson, 951, 1046
Davis, Mary Katherine, 427
Davis, Varina Howell, 952

# Indexes 159

Day, Kate Pickens, 903
Denny, William H., 632
De Rosier, Arthur H., 570, 571
Derrick, Samuel M., 695
Dexter, Franklin B., 432
Dix, John A., 589
Dodd, William E., 969
Doherty, Herbert J., 471
Donoghue, Frances J., 1054
Dorfman, Joseph, 1055
Downs, Robert B., 1135
Draper, Lyman C., 411
Drucker, Peter F., 1097
DuBose, John W., 904
Duffy, Bernard K., 1127
Dundas, F. de Sales, 412
Dunning, William A., 1080
Dyer, Oliver, 953

Easerby, J. Harold, 143, 437
Eaton, Clement, 472, 812
Edgar, Walter B., 491, 590
Edmunds, John B., 862
Edwards, Ninian W., 150
Eichert, Magdalen, 685, 686
Elliott, Charles Winslow, 821
Elliott, Edward G., 970
Ellis, Richard F., 633
Ellison, William H., 764
Elwell, Margaret Coit. *See* Coit, Margaret L.
Espy, James P., 581
Ethridge, Elizabeth W., 937
Eubanks, Ralph T., 1136
Ewing, Gretchen Garst, 607

Farmer, James O., 869
Faulkner, Ronnie W., 1099, 1100
Faunt, Joan Reynolds, 497
Faust, Drew Gilpin, 846
Featherstonhaugh, George W., 954
Federal Writers Project, 944
Fehrenbacher, Don E., 458, 775
Fischer, John, 1101
Fisher, Charles, 42
Fisher, George P., 433, 776
Fisher, John E., 675, 883
Fisher, Samuel Herbert, 438
Fitzhugh, George, 1068
Fitzsimmons, Matthew A., 704
Fleming, Thomas, 1102
Fletcher, Ralph Henry, 854

Flippin, Percy Scott, 35
Floyd, John, 151
Ford, Lacy K., 492, 1056, 1057
Fox-Genovese, Elizabeth, 905
Freehling, William W., 625, 656, 1081
Freidel, Frank, 853
Frothingham, Paul Revere, 722
Fulkerson, H. S., 764
Fuller, Margaret, 1160

Gabriel, Ralph Henry, 1006
Garber, Paul N., 842
Garnett, Muscoe R. H., 1007, 1047, 1137
Garraty, John A., 835
Garrison, George P., 98, 723
Garson, Robert A., 1069
Genovese, Eugene, 870, 1070
Gildersleeve, Basil L., 1048
Glenn, Virginia Louise, 844
Gliddon, George R., 1071
Godwin, Parke, 922, 1138
Gordon, Armistead C., 687
Gouverneur, Samuel L., 32
Govan, Thomas Payne, 807
Gower, Joseph F., 145
Graebner, Norman A., 724, 766, 767
Gray, Lewis Cecil, 473
Grayson, William John, 859, 1126
Green, Ben E., 634, 1058, 1059
Green, Duff, 141, 172, 189, 205, 212, 877
Green, Edwin L., 855
Green, Fletcher M., 474, 635, 636, 657, 658, 777, 778, 876, 878, 879, 880, 881
Greenberg, Kenneth S., 493
Greenhow, Robert, 753
Grund, Francis J., 955
Guess, William Francis, 483
Guilds, John C., 867
Gujer, Bruno, 725
Gunter, Michael M., 1100

Hall, Claude H., 893
Halley, Patrick L., 584
Hamer, Philip M., 779
Hamilton, Holman, 780
Hamilton, James A., 617
Hamilton, James, Jr., 366
Hamilton, Joseph G. de R., 839
Hamilton, Stanislaus M., 140

Hammond, Bray, 688
Hammond, George P., 100
Hammond, Jabez D., 735
Hammond, James Henry, 152, 153, 399, 847
Harden, Edward J., 91
Hargreaves, Mary W. M., 147, 608
Harp, Gillis J., 1029
Harris, J. William, 1082
Harrison, Lowell H., 400
Harrison, William Henry, 626
Hart, Albert Bushnell, 971
Hartz, Louis, 1008
Harwell, Donald Ray, 676
Hatch, Louis Clinton, 609
Hay, Thomas R., 36, 591
Hayne, Robert Y., 33
Head, Sylvia G., 937
Heale, M. J., 459
Healy, George P. A., 956
Hearon, Cleo, 659
Hecker, Isaac T., 145
Heckscher, Gunnar, 1083
Heitman, Francis B., 557
Hemphill, Susan L., 572
Hemphill, W. Edwin, 30, 545, 546, 547, 548, 549, 592, 593, 594, 1125
Henderson, William O., 754
Henry, Robert, 792
Herring, James, 974
Hill, C. William, 1030
Hill, Forrest G., 582
Hill, Lawrence F., 755
Hilliard, Henry W., 781
History Group, Inc., 906
Hizer, Trenton, 1172
Hofstadter, Richard, 1009
Hollis, Christopher, 1103
Holmes, Alester G., 907
Holst, Hermann E., von, 386, 994
Hopkins, James F., 147
Houston, David F., 660
Houston, Samuel, 154
Howe, George, 422
Howe, Henry, 925
Howell, Ronald, 641
Hubbell, Jay B., 1139
Huff, Archie Vernon, 836
Hunt, Gaillard, 387, 525, 961, 1140
Hunter, Martha T., 155
Hunter, Robert M. T., 137, 155, 388
Hutchinson, William T., 159

Hutton, Lawrence, 1167

Ingersoll, Charles Jared, 156, 526
Ingersoll, Ernest, 926
Ingersoll, L. D., 550
Ingham, William D., 885
Irving, Washington, 99

Jaccaud, Robert D., 945
Jackman, Sydney W., 37
Jackson, Andrew, 138, 157, 359
James, Edwin, 583
James, Marquis, 558, 677
Jameson, J. Franklin, 28, 428, 595
Janney, Samuel M., 736
Jeffrey, Robert C., 1104
Jenkins, John S., 389
Jenkins, William Sumner, 1072
Jennings, Thelma, 782
Jervey, Theodore D., 850
Johnson, Gerald W., 972
Johnson, Herschel V., 35
Johnson, Ludwell H., 783
Jollivet, Adolphe, 737
Jones, S. P., 938
Jones, Wilbur Devereux, 726
Joyner, Charles W., 509

Kaplanoff, Mark D., 445
Kateb, George, 1031
Kelly, J. R., 889
Kemper, Charles E., 414
Kendrick, Benjamin B., 401
Kennedy, John F., 521, 987, 992
Ketcham, Ralph, 819
Ketchum, Richard M., 1155
Kevlin, Thomas Anthony, 434
Kibler, Lillian Adele, 857
Kilbourne, Dwight C., 439
Kirk, Russell, 1010, 1105
Klein, Philip S., 596
Kuic, Vukan, 1106

Lambert, Oscar Doane, 705
Lander, Ernest M., 696, 768, 910, 911, 912, 913
Larkin, Thomas O., 100
Lathers, Richard, 39
Latimer, Margaret K., 527
Latner, Richard B., 618, 661
Leemhuis, Roger P., 856
Legaré, James M., 34

# Indexes

Leliart, Richard M., 145
Lerner, Ralph, 1011
Lesesne, J. Mauldin, 840
Lester, C. Edwards, 689
Levy, Naphtaly, 312
Lewis, Dixon H., 141
Lincoln, Abraham, 158
Lindsey, David, 390
Lloyd, Arthur Young, 460
Lodge, Henry Cabot, 973
Logan, John H., 423
Longacre, James B., 974
Longman, Philip, 1107
Longstreet, Augustus Baldwin, 170, 888, 975
Lovat-Fraser, J. A., 976
"Lowndes" (pseudonym), 690
Luraghi, Raimondo, 475
Lytle, Andrew, 977

McBride, Van Dyk, 1168
McCardell, John, 476
McCormick, Richard P., 461
McCoy, Drew R., 637
McDuffie, George, 42, 597
McFall, Pearl Smith, 927
McGee, Charles M., 913
McGrane, Reginald G., 144, 691
McKenney, Thomas L., 202, 573
McLaughlin, Andrew C., 638, 1013, 1141
McPherson, Lewin Dwinell, 416
McWilliams, Wilson C., 1014
Madison, James, 159
Magoon, E. L., 1142
Maier, Pauline, 662
Malone, Dumas, 837
Manning, William R., 101, 102
Marmor, Theodore, 1000, 1060
Martin, John M., 886
Martineau, Harriet, 957
Matthews, Steve A., 639
Maury, Sarah Mytton, 958
Maxcy, Virgil, 453, 595, 598, 706
Meigs, William M., 156, 391
Meleney, John C., 440
Meriwether, Robert L., 30, 424, 454
Merk, Frederick, 738
Merriam, Charles F., 1015
Merriman, John, 692
Merritt, Elizabeth, 848
Meyer, Isidore S., 756

Meyer, Leland M., 816
Middleton, Lamar, 614
Miles, Edwin A., 462, 515, 640
Miles, James Warley, 793
Mill, John Stuart, 1016
Miller, Arthur S., 641
Miller, Walter, 899
Mills, Robert, 484, 504
Minor, Lucian, 794
Mitchell, Broadus, 843
Mitchell, Franklin, 1084
Moltke-Hansen, David, 494, 510
Moltmann, Gunter, 41, 1085
Monroe, James, 140
Mooney, Chase C., 813
Moore, Alexander, 1127
Moore, Frederick W., 141, 875, 887
Moore, Glover, 540
Moore, John Bassett, 146
Moore, S. D., 795
Moore, W. Allan, Jr., 914
Moragné, Mary E., 915
Morgan, Robert J., 714
Morley, Felix, 1108, 1109
Morse, Howard N., 642
Morse, Jedidiah, 574
Moser, Harold D., 139, 157
Mouat, Linda, 947
Munroe, John A., 817
Musson, Eugéne, 1073

Nagel, Paul C., 643
National Portrait Gallery, 1152
Nevins, Allan, 163, 1169
Newmann, C. L., 928
Newsome, Albert Ray, 42
Nichols, Roger L., 584
Niven, John, 392, 828
Norwood, John Nelson, 739
Nott, Josiah C., 1071

O'Brien, Michael, 510, 851
Ochenkowski, John Paul, 663
Ogburn, Charlton, 1017
O'Neall, John Belton, 417, 441, 981
"Onslow" (pseudonym), 353–356
Owen, Thomas M., 43

Padover, Saul K., 978
Pakenham, Richard, 96
Pancake, John S., 822

Parish, John Carl, 693
Parker, Thomas Valentine, 575
Parks, E. Taylor, 757
Parrington, Vernon Louis, 1018
Parrish, William E., 784
Parton, James, 402
"Patrick Henry" (pseudonym), 610
Peake, Ora Brooks, 576
Pease, Jane H. and William, 664
Perkins, Dexter, 541
Perry, Benjamin F., 442, 495, 838, 841, 845, 979
Peterson, Merrill D., 393, 665
Peterson, Norma Lois, 715, 825
Petigru, James Louis, 858
Pfister, Harold Francis, 1156
Phifer, Robert S., 916
Phillips, Ulrich B., 161, 403, 477, 516
Pinckney, Charles C., 980
Pinckney, Gustavus M., 394
Pletcher, David A., 740
Polk, James K., 162, 163
Pollard, Edward A., 959
Porcher, Frederick A., 1161
Porter, Benjamin F., 981
Post, C. Gordon, 313, 1019
Potter, David M., 785, 1111
Pratt, Julius W., 528
Prentice, E. Parmalee, 1061
Preston, William C., 864
Preyer, Norris W., 535
Prior, Granville T., 496
Pritchett, John Perry, 982
Prucha, Francis Paul, 559, 560, 577

Rabun, James, 628
Raguet, Condy, 195, 209, 210
Rangila, Nancy A., 446
Raumer, Friedrich von, 960
Ravenel, Mrs. St. Julien, 522
Rawle, William, 1049
Rayback, Joseph G., 769
Reeves, Jesse Slidell, 727
Rell, Carl Lewis, 666
Rembert, Sarah H., 917
Remini, Robert V., 611, 620
Reynolds, Emily B., 497
Rhea, Linda, 852
Rhett, Robert Barnwell, 710, 711, 799, 1140
Richards, George H., 561
Richards, Leonard L., 805

Richards, Miles S., 697, 698, 1173
Ringgold, Mary Spencer, 948
Rippy, J. Fred, 863
Risjord, Norman K., 523
Ritzman, Carl H., 1143
Roback, Jennifer, 786
Robertson, Ben, 425
Roenne, Friedrich Ludwig von, 41
Rogers, George C., Jr., 443, 447, 485, 486, 511, 667, 699, 1112
Rogers, William W., 797
Roland, Charles P., 479
Romaine, Benjamin, 629
Röpke, Wilhelm, 1113
Rossiter, Clinton, 984, 1114
Ruffin, Edmund, 164
Rush, Richard, 985
Russell, Robert R., 478, 787
Rutledge, Anna Wells, 1154
Ryan, Halford R., 1127
Ryn, Claes G., 1115

Salley, Alexander S., 418, 419
Sanborn, Alvan F., 39
Sanders, George N., 44
Scafidel, James R., 888
Scarborough, William K., 164
Schafer, Joseph, 758
Schaper, William A., 498
Schlesinger, Arthur M., Jr., 463, 606, 679, 874, 1116
Schoolcraft, Henry R., 578
Scoville, Joseph A., 891, 900, 929
Schultz, Charles R., 700
Schultz, Harold S., 788, 986
Scott, Winfield, 562
Seager, Robert, II, 716
Seitz, Don C., 404
Sellers, Charles G., 820
Senese, Donald J., 1032
Seymour, Charles, 1170
Shalhope, Robert E., 1033, 1034, 1035
Shand, William M., 448
Shenton, James P., 830
Sherrill, George R., 907
Shipp, J. E. D., 149
Silbey, Joel H., 789
Silverthorne, Elizabeth, 741
Simkins, Francis Butler, 479
Simpson, Craig M., 834
Simpson, Richard W., 930

Simms, Henry Harrison, 884
Simms, William Gilmore, 165
Sioussat, St. George L., 728
Skeen, C. Edward, 600
Sloan, Dave M., 931
Smiley, David L., 1036
Smith, Alfred Glaze, 505
Smith, Ashbel, 742
Smith, Carlton B., 552
Smith, Joseph, 46
Smith, Justin H., 743
Smith, Margaret Bayard, 961
Smith, Whitefoord, 798
Smith, William E., 808
Smith, W. L. G., 810
Smither, Harriet, 744
Soulsby, Hugh G., 745
South Carolina Democratic Convention, 709
South Carolina General Assembly, 310, 799
South Carolina State Convention of 1832–1833, 627
Southwick, Leslie H., 405
Spain, August O., 1001
Spiller, Robert E., 1144
Spiller, Roger J., 553, 563, 564
Stampp, Kenneth M., 644
Stanwood, Edward, 668
Starke, William Pinkney, 428
Starr, Raymond G., 449
Steinberger, Peter J., 1117
Stenberg, Richard R., 621, 622, 669
Stephens, Alexander H., 1050
Stephenson, Nathaniel W., 529, 1020
Stevens, Sylvester K., 759
Stewart, James Brewer, 670
Stokes, Anson Phelps, 436
Stribling, J. C., 928
Styron, Arthur M., 395
Swift, Joseph G., 601, 602
Swisher, Carl Brent, 823
Sydnor, Charles S., 480
Symonds, G. W., 919

Tansill, Charles C., 760
Tarver, Jerry L., 1130
Taussig, Frank W., 1062
Taylor, Rosser H., 512
Thatcher, Harold W., 1086
Thomas, Emory M., 406
Thomas, John L., 989

Thomas, John Peyre, 800
Thompson, Henry T., 868
Thomson, Irving L., 890
Thornton, J. Mills, 517
Thornwell, James Henley, 801, 871
Thorpe, Thomas B., 1157
Tozawa, Kenji, 530, 790, 1021, 1174
Trent, William P., 990
Troup, George M., 91
Tucker, John Randolph, 1051
Tucker, Robert C., 849
Turnbull, Robert J., 630
Turner, Frederick Jackson, 464, 465, 542
Tyler, Lyon G., 166
Tyler, Samuel, 824

U.S. Congress, 89, 92, 93, 103, 104, 612, 796, 987, 988, 991, 992
Upshur, Abel P., 45, 1052
Upshur, John A., 45
Upton, Emory, 565

Van Buren, Martin, 829
Van Deusen, John G., 506
Viola, Herman J., 573, 579
Vipperman, Carl J., 524
"Virginian", 736
Volpe, Michael, 1145

Waddel, John Newton, 429
Wade, John Donald, 430
Wagstaff, Henry M., 518
Walker, Mary M., 1037
Walker, Robert J., 746
Wallace, David Duncan, 487
Walmsley, James E., 770
Walters, Raymond J., 536
Walton, Hanes, 1118
Waring, Alice N., 47
Watkins, F. T., 444
Watson, Margaret, 420
Weaver, Herbert H., 162
Weaver, Richard M., 645
Webster, Daniel, 168, 220, 796
Weigley, Russell F., 566
Weir, Robert M., 499, 500, 1038
Weisenburger, Francis P., 818
Weitenkampf, Frank, 1169
Welter, Rush, 466
Wentworth, John W., 962
Wesley, Edgar B., 567

Wharton, Francis, 1146
White, Henry A., 1147
White, Laura A., 865, 1087
White, Leonard D., 543
White, William S., 1119
Wick, Mildred Calhoun, 920
Wiesen, David S., 1074
Wikoff, Henry, 963
Wilkins, Joe B., 747
Williams, Amelia W., 154
Williams, Frances Leigh, 450
Williston, Ebenezer B., 222
Wilson, Clyde N., 30, 399, 407, 482, 613, 671, 672, 680, 681, 694, 712, 729, 730, 748, 749, 761, 847, 861, 882, 901, 933, 993, 994, 995, 996, 1022, 1039, 1075, 1120, 1148, 1175, 1176
Wilson, Major L., 646, 647, 682, 683
Wiltse, Charles M., 167, 168, 396, 467, 531, 603, 604, 673, 997, 1040, 1088, 1121, 1122
Wiltshire, Susan P., 1076
Winn, Larry James, 1149
Wise, Henry A., 717
Wolfe, John Harold, 451
Wood, Walter Kirk, 481, 1038
Woodward, Frank B., 811
Worsthorne, Peregrine, 1123

Yancey, William Lowndes, 802
Yarborough, Minnie Clare, 864
Yeates, W. S., 939
Young, Frances Packard, 554
Young, Klyde, 614
Young, Otis E., Jr., 940

Zeigel, Elizabeth, 1002
Zwicker, Dietrich, 1089

# SUBJECT INDEX

"AB Plot", 603
Abbeville District, S.C., 122, 301, 352, 411–413, 418, 427, 428, 906, 915
Aberdeen, Lord, 74
Abolitionism. *See* Slavery and abolitionism
Adams, John Quincy, 119, 142, 302, 303, 353–356, 590, 605–614, 803–805
Agrarians, Southern, 1090
Alabama, 10, 11, 43, 116, 306, 382, 517, 791, 795, 802, 886, 887, 904
Allston, Robert F. W., 143
American Revolution, 415, 449, 499, 1024, 1033–1036, 1041
Atchison, David R., 784

Banking. *See* Currency and banking
Bankruptcy law, 271
Belgium, 76
Benton, Thomas H., 223, 251, 292, 685, 806, 966
Biddle, Nicholas, 144, 807
Binney, Horace, 1064
Blair, Francis P., 808
Bluffton movement, 732, 749
Bonneau family, 914
Brady, Matthew, 1155–1157
Brazil, 76, 77, 338, 755
Brown, Jacob, 50
Brownson, Orestes A., 31, 128, 145, 206, 207, 873, 874
Buchanan, James, 146, 809
Burke, Aedanus, 440
Burt, Armistead, 9
Butler, Pierce M., 697

Caldwell family, 408, 415, 417
Calhoun College, Yale, 1170
Calhoun family, 409–420, 894, 897, 901–920

Calhoun Gold Mine, 934–940
Calhoun monument, Charleston, 967
Calhoun, Floride Colhoun (Mrs. John C.), 908, 911, 912, 914, 919
Calhoun, Patrick (grandfather), 419
Calhoun, Patrick (father), 415
Calhoun, Patrick (son), 912
California, 72, 100, 764
Canada, 101, 284, 751
Cass, Lewis, 810, 811
Census controversy, 349
Chappell family, 902
Charleston, S. C., 6, 174, 175, 304, 308, 370, 375, 437, 442, 443, 510, 699, 700, 793, 852, 967
Charleston *Mercury*, 175, 490, 496, 699
Cheves, Langdon, 836
Chile, 339
China, 77, 97
Clay, Henry, 131, 147, 148, 264, 274, 281, 393, 685, 724, 796, 812, 971, 972, 1132
Clemson, Anna Maria Calhoun, 917
Clemson, Floride Elizabeth, 913
Clemson, Thomas G., and family, 105, 907, 910
Cobb, Howell, 161
Colhoun family, 123
Colhoun, James Edward, 122, 906
Colombia, 77, 102, 757
Columbia, S.C., 176–178, 300, 792, 798, 799, 801, 917
Compromise of 1833, 283, 665
Compromise of 1850, 771–790
Concurrent majority, 217, 311–314, 383, 401, 671, 998–1022, 1029, 1031, 1037, 1083, 1084, 1091–1094, 1097–1108, 1110–1118, 1120–1123, 1135, 1174, 1175
Conner, Henry W., 6
Cooper, Thomas, 837

165

Crallé, Richard K., 106, 107, 141, 182, 311, 314, 875
Crawford, William H., 149, 585–587, 600, 604, 813
Crittenden, George B., 273
Cuba, 750
Cumming, William, 586
Currency and banking, 144, 240, 247, 248, 256, 261–266, 318, 376, 502, 533, 534, 536, 687, 688, 690, 691, 694, 807, 836, 840, 1054, 1058, 1059

Daguerreotypes, 1155–1157
Dahlonega, Ga., 934–940
Dallas, Alexander, J., 536
Dallas, George M., 588, 814
Davis, Warren R., 838
Defense, peacetime, 239, 320, 326, 330–332, 556, 563–566
Delaware, 817
De Saussure, Henry W., 437, 442
*Discourse on the Constitution and Government of the United States*, 217, 314
*Disquisition on Government*, 217, 311–313, 1007, 1135
Dix, John A., 589
Donelson, Andrew Jackson, 20, 350
Donelson, Emily, 616
Dorr War, 369
Douglass, David Bates, 37
Drayton, William Henry, 1024
Dumbarton Oaks, 944, 947
Dwight, Timothy, 432, 434

Eaton, Peggy, 363, 616, 619
Economic thought, Calhoun's, 997, 1000, 1053–1062, 1121. *See also* Currency and banking; Free trade and tariff; Public debt, expenditure, and revenue
Edgefield District, S.C., 179, 374, 376, 507
Edwards, Ninian, 7, 150
Elmore, Franklin H., 108, 109, 839–841
Everett, Edward, 73, 343, 348, 722
Exhumation of Calhoun's body during the Civil War, 943, 948

Fisher, Charles, 42
Fitzhugh, George, 1068–1070

Floyd, John, 151
"Fort Hill Address", 361, 362
Fort Hill plantation, 1, 894, 897, 901, 905, 907–910, 921–926, 929, 932, 933, 1148
France, 76, 77, 79, 295, 344, 371, 737, 1073, 1077, 1088, 1089
Free trade and tariff, 188, 195, 209, 210, 230, 235, 241, 260, 276, 282, 283, 309–310, 317, 368, 455, 501, 532, 535, 624, 626, 657, 668, 725, 1000, 1060, 1062, 1173

Gadsden, James, 842
Gales, Joseph, 525
Gardiner, John D., 9
Georgetown District, S.C., 511
Georgia, 10, 11, 35, 43, 91, 149, 161, 170, 171, 379, 516, 586, 587, 640, 655, 813, 934–940, 955, 960
Germany, 41, 76, 77, 342, 754, 1077, 1079, 1080, 1085, 1088
Gilmer, Thomas W., 38
Gold mine, Calhoun's, 934–940
Gordon, William Fitzhugh, 687
Gouverneur, Samuel L., 32, 129
Grayson, William John, 1126
Great Britain, 74, 76, 77, 79, 94–96, 101, 228–238, 270, 275, 284, 285, 315–317, 336, 343–345, 347, 348, 371, 689, 954, 957, 958, 726, 731, 740, 744, 745, 747, 752, 753, 758, 763, 766
Green, Ben E., 110, 876
Green, Duff, 110, 111, 141, 172, 189, 205, 212, 226, 607, 877–882, 1173
Greenhow, Robert, 730
Greenwood County, S.C., 420
Gregg, William, 843
Gwin, William M., 764

Hall, Bolling, 10
Hamilton, James, Jr., 365, 366, 666, 844, 845
Hammond, James H., 132, 152, 153, 846–849
Harper, William, 639
Harrison, William Henry, 626, 715
Hawaii, 77, 759
Hayne, Robert Y., 33, 645, 658, 700, 850
Hegel, G. W. F., 1083
Hobbes, Thomas, 1078

# Indexes

House of Representatives, Calhoun in, 49, 120, 218, 224, 228–243, 315–318, 454, 519–536
Houston, Samuel, 154
Hunter, Robert M. T., 112–114, 137, 155, 675, 883, 884, 1125, 1140

Illinois, 7, 46, 150, 158
Indians, 54–56, 89, 91, 319, 324, 327, 328, 568–579, 640
Ingersoll, Charles J., 156, 526
Ingham, Samuel D., 885
Instruction of representatives, 242
Internal improvements, 33, 243, 307, 321, 332, 335, 351, 582, 692, 695, 700, 1054
Interposition. *See* Nullification
Iowa, 693
Irving, Washington, 99

Jackson, Andrew, 69, 115, 138, 139, 157, 247, 250–253, 256, 333, 358–360, 390, 558, 607, 611, 615–622, 644, 652, 661, 669, 671, 677, 724, 815
Jefferson, Thomas, 21, 448, 1023, 1030, 1034, 1058, 1077, 1103
Jesup, Thomas S., 51
Johnson, Herschel V., 35
Johnson, Richard M., 816
Jones, George W., 693

Kentucky, 44, 816
King, Charles Bird, 1151
King, Martin Luther, 1118
King, William R., 344, 371

Larkin, Thomas O., 72, 100
Law practice, Calhoun's, 8, 437–444
Legaré, Hugh S., 851, 852
Legaré, James M., 34
Lewis, Dixon H., 116, 141, 886, 887
Library, Calhoun's, 945, 946
Lieber, Francis, 17, 853
*Life of John C. Calhoun* (1843), 388, 1125, 1131, 1137, 1140
Lincoln, Abraham, 158, 941, 942, 964, 1103
Litchfield Law School, 438, 439
Long, Stephen H., 580, 583, 584
Longstreet, A. B., 170, 430, 888, 975
Louisiana, 183, 208
Lowndes, William, 120, 522, 524

MacBride, James, 22
McDuffie, George, 42, 127, 586, 597, 854, 855
McKenney, Thomas L., 202, 573, 579
McLane, Louis, 817
McLean, John, 23, 818
McLeod, Alexander, 275
Macomb, Alexander, 561
Madison, James, 159, 519, 520, 637, 819, 1037, 1056, 1078
Mallory, Francis, 368
Marshall, John, 640, 1109
Marxism, 1009
Maryland, 25, 117, 172, 211, 595, 598, 822, 889, 890
Massachusetts, 5, 119, 173, 206, 514
Mathewes, John R., 18
Maxcy, Virgil, 117, 595, 598, 889, 890
Memorials, 791–802
Memphis Memorial, 306, 351
Methodists, 739, 798
Mexican War, 287–289, 292–294, 296, 373, 762, 767, 768
Mexico, 72, 76, 77, 79, 100, 110, 341, 346
Michigan, 180, 257, 703
Mills, Clark, 1158, 1167
Mississippi, 181, 515, 653, 659, 765, 830
Missouri, 784
Missouri Compromise, 540, 605
Monroe, James, 32, 53, 118, 129, 130, 140, 160, 537–543
Monroe Doctrine, 538, 541
Mormons, 46
Morton, Marcus, 5
Moynihan, Daniel P., 1100

Newberry District, S.C., 408, 417
Newspapers, 169–205
New York, 9, 169, 184–189, 207, 213, 214, 377, 378, 601, 617, 679, 702, 707, 835
Noble family, 410
Noble, Patrick, 47
North Carolina, 42, 518, 597, 941
Norvell, John, 335
Nullification; as doctrine, 244–246, 309, 310, 357, 361, 362, 364–367, 613, 631–647; as historical episode, 151, 152, 177, 244–246, 304, 374, 375, 648–673, 844, 1136; documents of, 623–630

Ohio, 23, 194, 380, 381, 626, 818, 949
Oratory. *See* Speeches, Calhoun's
Oregon, 96, 285, 286, 297, 345, 347, 694, 723, 724, 727, 740, 752, 753, 758, 763, 766
Orr, James L., 774, 856

Pakenham, Richard, 74, 96, 336, 345, 347
Patronage, abuses of, 251, 252, 287, 333, 1081
Pendleton, S.C., 190, 303, 305, 921, 927, 928, 930, 931
Pennsylvania, 15, 146, 156, 195, 209, 210, 534, 588, 596, 814, 885, 985, 1042, 1049, 1056, 1064
Periodicals, 206–214
Perry, Benjamin F., 857, 975, 979
Petigru, James L., 858–861
Pickens, Andrew, Jr., 9
Pickens, Francis W., 40, 124, 862
Pickens family, 903, 916
Pinckney, Henry Laurens, 699
Pinckney family, 443, 450
Poinsett, Joel R., 863
Polk, James K., 133, 162, 163, 294, 704, 724, 727, 740, 762, 763, 766–768, 820
Portraits, 1150–1154
Powers, Hiram, 1160–1162
Presbyterians, 422. *See also* Thornwell, James H.
Presidency, power of, 250–252, 280, 294, 333, 380, 997. *See also* Patronage, abuses of
Presidential candidacy (1824), 36, 42, 117, 202, 463, 539, 585–604, 813.
Presidential candidacy (1844), 117, 145, 180, 186, 189, 203, 370, 380, 381, 463, 701–712
Preston, William C., 696, 697, 864
Public debt, expenditure, and revenue, 231, 260, 261, 269, 273, 274, 276–279, 281, 282, 317, 684
Public lands, 158, 259, 267, 272–274, 277, 278, 335, 685, 686, 694, 1054

Raguet, Condy, 195, 209, 210
Railroads, 33, 695, 700
Randolph, John, 228, 1010
Religion, 422, 739, 798, 869–871, 900, 1027, 1092

Revolutions of 1848, 295, 1077, 1079, 1085, 1088
Rhett, Robert Barnwell, 121, 490, 732, 799, 865, 1140
Rip Rap contract, 606, 612
Ritchie, Thomas, 513
Rives, William C., 134
Röenne, Friedrich Ludwig, von, 41
Roman influences on Calhoun, 1026, 1074, 1076, 1084
Ruffin, Edmund, 164
Rush, Richard, 15

Sanders, George N., 44
Santo Domingo, 760
Schoolcraft, Henry R., 24, 578
Scott, Winfield, 562, 821
Scoville, Joseph A., 891
Sculpture, 1158–1162
Seddon, James A., 125, 892
Seminole War controversy, 32, 358–360, 558, 617, 621, 622
Senate, Calhoun in, 70, 88, 162, 163, 200, 218, 221, 225–227, 244–299, 333–335, 351, 674–700, 762–790, 1119
Senators, Calhoun as one of the five great, 987, 992
Shannon, Wilson, 341, 346
Silhouette of Calhoun, 1163
Silliman, Benjamin, 433
Simkins family, 916, 918
Simms, William Gilmore, 165, 866, 867
Slavery and abolitionism, 185, 254, 255, 258, 270, 290, 291, 298, 299, 308, 334, 343, 344, 348, 349, 371–373, 460, 469, 470, 472, 481, 509, 605, 649, 656, 689, 693, 725, 731–749, 771–790, 1063–1076, 1128, 1130, 1133
Smith, Ashbel, 741, 742
Smith, Joseph, 46
Smith, Samuel, 25, 822
Smith, William, 369
Smith, William Loughton, 447
South: history and description, 468–480
Southard, Samuel L., 16
South Carolina: history and description, 408–430, 440, 441, 443, 482–512, 1004, 1024–1027, 1032, 1038,

1039, 1087, 1091, 1112; memorials to Calhoun, 792, 793, 798–801; newspapers, 174–179, 190, 490, 496; politics, 6, 9, 33, 40, 42, 47, 48, 108, 109, 120, 121, 124, 127, 132, 143, 152, 153, 165, 300, 301, 303, 305, 308, 352, 370, 375, 376, 383, 399, 452–454, 461, 522, 524, 527, 709, 732; politics after Calhoun, 772–774, 779, 788; politics before Calhoun, 445–451; politics post-Nullification, 680, 681, 695–700; public figures contemporary to Calhoun, 836–872. *See also* Nullification
South Carolina Constitution, 383
*South Carolina Exposition,* 309, 310, 635
South Carolina General Assembly, 48, 309, 310, 357, 364, 367, 488, 491, 497, 698, 799
Spain, 79, 99
Speeches, Calhoun's, 215–308, 1124–1149
Spoils. *See* Patronage, abuses of
State debts, 269
State Department, Calhoun as Secretary of, 4, 20, 41, 71–87, 94–104, 110, 135, 154, 156, 166, 200, 219, 336–350, 382, 713–761, 834
State rights, 244–246, 249, 257, 268, 269, 275, 299, 309, 310, 314, 369, 466, 477, 481, 516, 518, 629, 978, 982, 1023–1026, 1028, 1033–1035, 1038–1052, 1086, 1087, 1095, 1108, 1115, 1120, 1143, 1144. *See also* Nullification
Statuary Hall, Calhoun in, 988
Stephens, Alexander H., 161
Subtreasury, 263–266
Surplus revenue, 684
Swift, Joseph G., 601, 602

Tait, Charles, 11, 43
Taney, Roger B., 823, 824
Tariff. *See* Free trade and tariff
Taylor, John, 1029, 1030
Tazewell, Littleton W., 18, 825
Tennessee, 306, 616, 650
Texas, 4, 20, 38, 45, 71, 76, 77, 79, 98, 154, 337, 340, 344, 350, 723–725, 727, 729, 731–736, 738–746, 749
Thompson, Waddy, 868
Thornwell, James H., 869–871
Tocqueville, Alexis de, 1077
Toombs, Robert, 161
Troup, George M., 91
Townes family, 126
Treaty-making power, 238
Turney, Hopkins L., 289
Tyler, John, 86, 135, 166, 200, 280, 337, 713–717, 727, 740

United Nations, 1084, 1099, 1100
U.S. Military Academy, 37, 59, 60, 322, 325, 555
Upshur, Abel P., 45, 718, 893, 1052

Van Buren, Martin, 86, 136, 169, 199, 263, 376–378, 392, 611, 617, 620, 681, 682, 704, 826–829, 835
Vandeventer, Christopher, 3, 26
Vice President, Calhoun as, 68–69, 227, 302, 303, 353–356, 358–360, 605–622
Virginia, 18, 106, 107, 112–114, 125, 134, 137, 151, 155, 166, 182, 191–193, 368, 369, 513, 637, 675, 687, 717, 718, 736, 825, 834, 875, 883, 884, 892, 893, 1045, 1052

Waddel, Moses, 426, 429, 430
Walker, Robert J., 746, 830
War Department, Calhoun as secretary of, 24, 50–67, 89–93, 115, 118, 119, 140, 154, 219, 319–332, 537–584, 600, 603, 604, 811, 813, 816
War of 1812, 228–237, 315–317, 352, 454, 519, 525–531, 1149
Washington newspapers, 195–205
Webster, Daniel, 167, 168, 246, 265, 274, 284, 393, 645, 658, 685, 724, 776, 796, 831, 832, 971, 972
Webster-Hayne debate, 645, 658
West Indies, 747, 750, 760
West Point, 37, 59, 60, 322, 325, 555
Wheaton, Henry, 13, 342, 833
Williams, David R., 872
Wilson, Woodrow, 1103

Wise, Henry A., 338, 717, 834
Wright, Silas, 835

Yale College, 9, 12, 22, 431–436, 1170
Yancey, William L., 904

Yellowstone expedition, 323, 580, 583, 584
Yucatan, 296

Zionism, 756

# SERIAL PUBLICATIONS

Alabama Historical Quarterly
Alfred University Studies
American Antiquarian Society Proceedings
American Bar Association Journal
American Heritage
American Historical Association Annual Report
American Historical Review
American History Illustrated
American Political Science Quarterly
Anderson, S.C., Daily Mail
Antioch Review
Antiques
Boston, Mass., Post
Brownson's Quarterly Review
Bucks County Historical Society Papers
California Historical Society Quarterly
Camden, S.C., Journal
Carolina Planter
Carologue
Casket
Charleston, S.C., Courier
Charleston, S.C., Mercury
Christian Science Monitor
Chronicles of Culture
Cincinnati, Ohio, Daily Enquirer
Cincinnati, Ohio, Daily Gazette
Civil War History
Columbia, S.C., State
Comparative Studies in Society and History
Congressional Record
Continuity
Dartmouth College Library Bulletin
De Bow's Review
Diplomatic History
Edgefield, S.C., Advertiser
Ehime Law Journal
Ehime Law Review
Emory University Quarterly
Encounter
Geological Survey of Georgia Bulletin
Georgia Historical Quarterly
Georgia Review
Green Bag
Gulf States Historical Magazine
Harper's
Harper's New Monthly Magazine
Harvard Law Review
The Historian
Historica
Human Events
Iustitua
Jahrbuch fur Amerikastudien
Journal of American History
Journal of Mississippi History
Journal of Politics
Journal of Public Law
Journal of Southern History
Journal of the Early Republic
Journal of the History of Ideas
Ladies' Home Journal
Lippincott's Monthly
Living Age
London Quarterly Review
Manuscripts
Maryland Historical Magazine
Michigan Law Review
Mississippi Historical Society Publications
Mississippi Valley Historical Review
Mobile, Ala., Register and Journal
Modern Age
Nation
Nation's Business
Newberry, S.C., Observer
New England Journal of Public Policy
New York, N.Y., Citizen
New York, N.Y., Evening Post
New York, N.Y., Herald
New York Public Library Bulletin
XIX Century
North American Review
North Carolina Historical Review
Oregon Historical Society Quarterly
Pendleton, S.C., Messenger

Philadelphia, Pa., Franklin Gazette
Political Science Quarterly
Polity
Public Administration Review
Publications of the Southern History Association
Publius
The Rambler
Review of Politics
Scribner's Magazine
Scribner's Monthly
Scripps College Papers
South Atlantic Quarterly
South Carolina Bar Association Transactions
South Carolina Historical Association Proceedings
South Carolina Historical Magazine
South Carolina History Illustrated
South Carolina Law Quarterly
South Carolina Reveiw
Southern Historical Society Papers
Southern Humanities Review
Southern Literary Messenger
Southern Living
Southern Partisan
Southern Quarterly Review
Southern Review (old)
Southern Review (new)
Southern Speech Communication Journal
Southwestern Historical Quarterly
Spartanburg, S.C., Carolina Spartan
Staats-und-völkerrechtliche Abhandlungen
Teaching Political Science
Tennessee Historical Quarterly
Time
Transactions of the Huguenot Society of South Carolina
Tulane Law Review
Tyler's Historical Magazine
United States Magazine and Democratic Review
University of Chicago Record
Virginia Magazine of History and Biography
Virginia Quarterly Review
Washington, D.C., United States' Telegraph
Washington Monthly
Washington University Studies
William and Mary Quarterly
Wisconsin Magazine of History
World and I
Yale Literary Magazine